Great Palaces

Great
Palaces

D.M. Field

WINDWARD

Photographic acknowledgments
The photographs on pages 14, 16–17, 20 bottom, are reproduced by gracious permission of Her Majesty The Queen.

Aéro-Photo, Paris 34 bottom; Boudot-Lamotte, Paris 7 top, 10, 59 bottom, 126; British Tourist Authority, London 11, 13, 21, 23; J. Allen Cash, London 87, 94, 103 top, 103 bottom, 105, 107; Colour Library International, London 8, 12, 28 bottom, 29, 41, 52, 53, 57, 60, 65, 88, 89 top, 96–7, 109 bottom, 112, 116–17, 124–5; Country Life, London 14, 18 bottom; Danish Tourist Board, London 104; Photographie Giraudon, Paris 24 top, 24 bottom, 25, 30, 32–3, 40 top, 40 bottom, 43, 44 top, 44 bottom, 45 top, 45 bottom; Hamlyn Group Picture Library front cover, endpapers, 36 top, 47, 61, 106; Michael Holford, Loughton 28 top, 92 bottom, 93 top, 93 bottom; Angelo Hornack, London 26, 73; Camilla Jessel, Twickenham 99; A. F. Kersting, London 7 bottom, 15, 22, 38, 48–9, 64, 66, 68–9, 90, 95; Mansell Collection, London 70, 71, 74 top, 74 bottom, 75, 78, 79 top, 79 bottom, 82, 83 top, 86; Bildarchiv Foto Marburg 54, 55, 59 top, 62 top, 62 bottom, 63; John Massey Stewart, London 118, 119 bottom, 122, 123; Musées Nationaux, Paris 6; Netherlands Information Service – Bart Hofmeester 110, 111, 113 top, 113 bottom, 114; Novosti Press Agency, London 115, 119 top; Rheinisches Bildarchiv Stadtmuseum, Cologne 50, 51; Jean Roubier, Paris 35, 46, 58; Scala, Antella back cover, 72 left, 72 right, 76 top, 76 centre, 76 bottom, 77 top, 77 bottom, 81, 83 bottom, 84–5; Scottish Tourist Board, Edinburgh 20 top; Spanish Tourist Board, London 91; Spanish Tourist Board – John Hedgecoe 89 bottom; Spectrum, London 120–1; Tony Stone Associates, London 92 top, 108 top, 108 bottom; Wim Swaan, New York 67, 80 bottom, 98, 102; Swedish Tourist Board, Stockholm 109 top; Judy Todd, London 18 top; Roger Viollet, Paris 27, 31, 34 top, 39, 42; Vision International, London 80 top; Warburg Institute, London 19; ZEFA (UK), London – Dr. David Corke 127; ZEFA (UK), London – V. Phillips 100–1; ZEFA (UK), London – H. Schumacher 9; ZEFA (UK), London – G. Seider 56; ZEFA (UK), London – P. J. Sharpe title spread; ZEFA (UK), London – Ronald Sheridan 36 bottom; ZEFA (UK), London – F. Walther 37.

Front cover:	The Escorial, Spain
Back cover:	Caserta, Italy
Endpapers:	Blenheim Palace, England
Title spread:	The Belvedere, Austria

728.82

2 893662

Copyright © The Hamlyn Publishing Group Limited 1982
London · New York · Sydney · Toronto
Astronaut House, Feltham, Middlesex, England

Published in this edition by Windward, an imprint owned by W H Smith and Son Limited. Registered No 237811 England.

Trading as WHS Distributors, St John's House, East Street, Leicester, LE1 6NE

ISBN 0 711 20230 3

Printed in Italy

CONTENTS

Introduction

The palace – the home of a royal or princely court – reached its height in Europe in the 17th and 18th centuries, at a time when most countries were ruled by dynastic sovereigns whose powers – in principle if not always in practice – were almost absolute. This was the age of the 'enlightened despot', the ruler whose near-despotic authority over his (or her) subjects was tempered by reformist ideas and, usually, enthusiastic patronage of the arts. The essential purpose of the palaces they erected was to glorify their own rule, dazzling their subjects and, if possible, disconcerting their jealous rivals. It is no coincidence that the most grandiose monarch in European history was also the builder of the grandest palace – Versailles.

Of course, the desire of powerful rulers to display their prestige by the splendour of their court and the majesty of their residences was not confined to this short period. It is characteristic of all societies as far back as archaeology can show. The rulers of ancient Egypt, Assyria and Persia lived in large and luxurious buildings, and the palace of King Minos at Knossos in Crete is a famous example of this ancient tradition. Outstanding examples from the Classical era still survive, in Hadrian's Villa near Rome and at Split in Yugoslavia, in a sufficiently well-preserved state for the most detailed models to be constructed of their original appearance. The palace of Split was built in the early 4th century AD by the Emperor Diocletian as a symbol of his efforts to reunite and reinvigorate the Roman Empire, though eventually Diocletian gave up the task and announced his intention of retiring to Split to grow vegetables. The successors of many of the builders of the great European palaces have similarly descended to less glorious occupations though, unlike Diocletian, the choice was not often their own.

Several other great palaces were erected in the late Roman period. One of the most splendid was founded in the Emperor Constantine's new capital in the 4th century. At its grandest, under the Byzantine emperors five or six centuries later, it included every imaginable luxury, including mechanical singing birds in artificial trees – a favourite device of other Eastern potentates, such as Harun al-Raschid. The palace of Constantinople was sacked by the unruly Crusaders in 1204 and the site subsequently built over by the Turks; only a few chips of sculpture and mosaic have survived.

The semi-tribal chiefs of early medieval Europe often built vast wooden halls where noisy ceremonies and banquets took place. The royal hall at Tara near Dublin appears to have been some 200 metres (650 feet) long. The Great Hall continued to be a feature of palaces throughout the Middle Ages and, indeed, into later times. Charlemagne's palace at Aachen, the chapel of which still stands, was centred on a great hall, though it also included other elements derived from imperial Rome.

Versailles, seen here in a 17th-century painting by Pierre Patel the Elder, is the most deliberately grand of all great European royal palaces. Its vast acres proclaim the glory of absolute monarchy in France, and it inspired lesser monarchs with similar architectural ambitions.

Very few palaces from medieval Europe have survived, partly because few were built (one exception is the imperial palace at Goslar in Lower Saxony). And the reason they were not built – because they were likely to be destroyed by hostile neighbours or rebellious subjects – also explains why those that were built have long since perished. From about the 9th to the 15th century, in most of Europe the residences of kings and lesser rulers were not palaces but fortified castles, built for security rather than comfort. Of course there was no reason why the interior apartments should not be comfortable as well as safe, and no doubt some of them were as luxurious as any palace.

This brings us to the problem of definition. What, exactly, is a 'palace'? The word derives from the Latin *palatium*, the Palatine Hill in Rome, where imperial residences were built in the late Roman period. A palace is, therefore, first and foremost a splendid dwelling place. Other characteristics, however, are less definite. Generally speaking, a palace is more than a residence, it is a centre of power, accommodating officials and servants and state rooms for public functions. Typically, the inhabitant of a palace is a ruler of some kind, though the word is often applied on grounds of size and

7

François I's fairy palace, the Château de Chambord, one of the most astonishing of all Renaissance buildings. Strict critics might quibble at its riotous roofline, making such a contrast with the appearance of Classical order below, but it remains one of the most distinctive of all rural palaces.

grandeur to other buildings usually occupied by someone who, if not the actual ruler, held a powerful position in the state.

Castles fulfil these qualifications, but they are fortified buildings whereas palaces are not. The dividing line between them is often unclear, and the matter is complicated by the fact that many castles were turned into palaces in later times, though without sacrificing their towers and battlements. For the purpose of this book, such buildings are generally excluded, though a few exceptions have been made where the remaining fortifications form only a small part of the whole.

Other difficulties arise in other languages. In France, for example, the word *château*, which in English is translated as 'castle', is often loosely applied to a variety of buildings, ranging from a fortress to a country villa, but in particular to residences which in England would be called country houses.

By the time of the Renaissance, castles were becoming redundant. Gunpowder and artillery made them far less impregnable, while, more important, royal governments which had achieved greater power in their dominions had less to fear from rebellious subjects. Europe became, in strictly relative terms, more peaceful, and although a great many palaces in modern Europe have perished at the hands of angry men, on the whole their greatest enemy has been not the deliberate act of man but the accidental outbreak of fire.

The first Renaissance palaces were built by the leading families of the North Italian cities, and they retained a certain fortress-like appearance, though characterized by Classical rules of order and proportion as well as Classical ornament of columns and round arches. In the 16th century, these town palaces became grander. The Palazzo Farnese in Rome is a highly elaborate, perfectly integrated complex (although Michelangelo's ambitious scheme was never entirely completed). Meanwhile, in the Venetian Republic, Andrea Palladio, whose influence was to be so wide-ranging, incorporated the imposing Classical motifs of pediment and dome in his rural villas.

The new ideas of palace-building spread rapidly abroad, finding an enthusiastic champion in François I, whose remarkable palaces at Fontainebleau and Chambord were the marvels of the age, while in Spain, Charles V's palace in Granada showed a complete mastery of the principles of the Italian Renaissance.

The Baroque age, from the late 16th to the 18th century, was the great age of palace building. Again, Italy was the pioneer, and architects from other countries eagerly studied the ideas of Carlo Maderno, Gian Lorenzo Bernini and Carlo Fontana. However, Bernini's plans for the Louvre in Paris were rejected, a sign that France was about to seize the cultural initiative. Versailles, built for Louis XIV, established the supremacy of French designers like Delorme, Le Vau, Le Nôtre (the celebrated landscape gardener), the artist Le Brun and Mansart. Jealousy inspired other monarchs to emulate Versailles, though they had to be content with less splendid versions.

In Germany the Baroque style took on a new character in the hands of architects like Fischer von Erlach, Balthasar Neumann and Lucas von Hildebrandt, while some of the most attractive of all Baroque buildings were created for the smaller states of southern Germany towards the end of the period.

The French Revolution brought all this extravagance to an end. Although some palaces were built in the 19th century, they were exceptional, like the fantastic exercises in royal nostalgia in which Ludwig of Bavaria indulged. Royal autocracy persisted in Russia and a few other countries, but it was increasingly difficult for any ruler to get away with such showmanship. Versailles was seen as an insult to the French people, and it is surprising that the mobs left a stone standing.

Anyone contemplating the great palaces of Europe today must experience mixed emotions: admiration for craftsmen and artists, and perhaps their employers: nostalgia for a bygone age possibly, when the display of great wealth was not considered morally suspect; but

The Gallery of Mirrors at Ludwig II's Schloss Herrenchiemsee, a white elephant of a place constructed for a king whose hobby of palace-building had become, by the 19th century, a slightly grotesque anachronism.

The Great Staircase of the Würzburg
Residenz, which has been called the most
splendid staircase in Europe. More than one
visitor has fallen flat on his face through fixing
his eyes on Tiepolo's brilliantly painted
ceiling.

inevitably too a slight feeling of
disgust at such ostentatious expendi-
ture by the great when the lowly
existed in such comparative squalor.
As a corrective, it might be pointed
out that the gap in living standards
between the palace and the hovel in
the 18th century was probably no
greater than separates a middle-class
household in Western Europe or
North America today from the poor
of many Third World countries.

Disenchantment may take a more
immediate form. Would you really
want a Louis XV commode in your
living room, or a Tiepolo on the
dining-room ceiling? And those
stately staircases. How dreadful if
you needed to go upstairs in a hurry.

Although English monarchs, with
smaller revenue and greater limits on
their authority, built no royal palaces
as grand as those of France or Spain,

Queen Victoria, seated on her little
chair amid the vast expanse of the
state drawing rooms in Buckingham
Palace or Windsor Castle, used to
sigh for the simple life and a country
cottage. Such thoughts must have
strayed into many a crowned head,
condemned to live in some such
mighty shrine as Schönbrunn or the
royal palace at Naples. Napoleon,
who stayed in more great palaces
than anyone, seems to have been
most comfortable at Malmaison,
more country house than palace.

Today, nearly everyone's living
quarters are growing smaller, and it
takes an effort of imagination to
comprehend life on the old scale. The
effort is, of course, well worth
making, and whether you are more
struck by the beauty of the frescoes or
the absence of bathrooms, there is
always plenty to see and wonder at.

Palaces of the British Isles

Blenheim Palace

Blenheim Palace, according to Sir John Summerson, is 'almost the only English plan which has found its way into a French textbook [of architecture]'. This is a paradox in more ways than one. To a certain extent Blenheim represents a deliberate jibe at France: it is a monument to the Duke of Marlborough, victor over the French armies at the Battle of Blenheim in 1704, and a simultaneous assertion that the French were not the only people who could build a grand Baroque palace.

It was, after all, the style of Sir Christopher Wren, and as he was still in his prime when Queen Anne (prompted, no doubt, by her bosom pal, the Duchess of Marlborough) decided to build her victorious general a palace at state expense, it is a little surprising that the Duke did not choose Wren as architect. Instead he chose Sir John Vanbrugh, a slightly rakish, aristocratic ex-soldier and author of at least two very funny comedies (*The Provoked Wife* and *The Relapse*). He had already been chosen to design Castle Howard in Yorkshire, and both there and at Blenheim he co-operated with Nicholas Hawksmoor, the English architect whose reputation in recent years has risen more sharply than almost any other. Both were men of genius, which makes it suprising they co-operated so well. Vanbrugh in fact eventually walked out, after endless rows with the Duchess, and the self-effacing Hawksmoor finished the job – never, apparently, receiving his full fee.

The dominant features of the palace are the four bulky towers of the main complex and the unusual entrance portico where, behind the Classical pediment, a second, higher pediment appears over the main hall. The skyline is a rich and imaginative sculptural array by Grinling Gibbons and others, and the whole building is in the golden stone of Oxfordshire. It is very much an architect's building, and the interior,

except for the elegant Long Library (originally intended as an art gallery) is not especially memorable.

The great parterre laid out under Vanbrugh's direction in the French manner disappeared later in the 18th century when the park was 'anglicized' by 'Capability' Brown (who created the lake). The 9th Duke (1871–1934), who is largely responsible for the fine condition of the palace today, compensated for this by creating smaller formal gardens to the north and south.

The massive Saloon at Blenheim Palace, with frescoes by a French artist, Louis Laguerre – an appropriate name for the decorator of a general's palace.

Right: Plastic fruit in the Banqueting Hall of the Royal Pavilion augments the air of amiable fraudulence that hangs about this richly exotic building.

Below: The cupolas of Brighton Pavilion. A contemporary wit, unimpressed by this oriental extravaganza, remarked that the dome of St Paul's Cathedral had 'gone down to Brighton and pupped'.

Brighton Pavilion

English monarchs have not, on the whole, indulged in architectural extravagances. The one outstanding exception is the delightful if frivolous Oriental fantasy of the Prince Regent (later George IV) known as Brighton Pavilion.

The rise of Brighton as England's most fashionable seaside resort was due mainly to the Prince, who first visited it in 1783 and built a brick villa there, small but exquisite, some years later. About 1800 he decided to extend the villa. One of the additions was a riding school, a domed building in a style described as 'Saracenic', and in 1806 Humphrey Repton, better known as a landscape gardener, was called in to submit plans to transform the pavilion. Repton had recently been consulted about a house in Oxfordshire for a retired nabob of the East India Company, and had 'discovered new sources of beauty and variety' in Indian architecture. This new enthusiasm, plus the appearance of the riding school, resulted in designs based on 'the architecture of Hindustan'. The Prince was delighted, but Repton's finances then took a turn for the worse and when work began ten years later it was the fashionable John Nash, not the unfortunate Repton, who gained the commission.

Nash's building is hardly Indian or, indeed, in any other known style, though it is indisputably and extravagantly 'Oriental' in flavour. The interior presents the best collection of *chinoiserie* in England, and possibly the best Regency furniture. The exterior has a suggestion of a pantomime back-drop, with its sparkling white domes, minarets, fretted balconies and creamy walls. The Pavilion aroused much popular interest, and in the 19th century was pictured in books more often than any other English building. Today it is a national treasure.

The Grand Staircase of Buckingham Palace, above which Perseus threatens to drop the Gorgon's head on those passing below.

Buckingham Palace

Compared with her medieval predecessors, the present Queen of England is poorly provided with palaces. She has only three official ones, Buckingham Palace, Windsor Castle and Holyrood House, and two private houses, Balmoral and Sandringham. Buckingham Palace, in the heart of London, has been the principal residence of the sovereign for about one hundred years. It is a comparatively modern building: the familiar east front facing the Mall was completed only seventy years ago, and although parts of an earlier building are incorporated, the Palace can hardly be said to be older than John Nash's restructuring in the early 19th century. It derives its name from the original owner of what was then Buckingham House, whose descendant sold it to George III in 1762.

When George IV came to the throne in 1820 he commissioned Nash to extend the house. Nash did a great deal to make London a more beautiful city, but it cannot be said that Buckingham Palace is an architectural masterpiece. The garden front, handsome despite a rather coy dome, is perhaps Nash's best work, apart from the Grand Staircase. Two pavilions, suggesting Classical temples, were regarded as unsightly and were pulled down, while the Triumphant Arch at the entrance was later shifted to its present position at the north-east corner of Hyde Park (Marble Arch).

The first monarch to live there was Queen Victoria, who announced her decision to move in with alacrity, being anxious to escape her mother's circle at Kensington Palace. Though pleased with it, she later commanded considerable alterations.

Probably the most magnificent room is the Blue Drawing Room (formerly the Ball Room), containing Napoleon's Sèvres porcelain table with portraits of military heroes and a clock designed by George III (with a little help from his friends). Many paintings from the royal collection are on public view in the Queen's Gallery, and the public may also inspect the state coaches in the Royal Mews.

Overleaf: The Blue Drawing Room at Buckingham Palace.

The main façade of Buckingham Palace, with the Victoria Memorial in front. The building is perhaps at its best with large, cheering crowds round about and the royal family waving gracefully from a beribboned balcony.

Right: The Great Gatehouse of Hampton Court Palace, with heraldic beasts and 'Tudor' chimneys. The rather virulent appearance of the recently renewed brickwork will mellow in course of time.

Below: The garden façade, part of the additions to Hampton Court made by Sir Christopher Wren. The course of circular windows faintly echoes a motif seen at St Paul's Cathedral.

Hampton Court

Hampton Court, England's nearest equivalent to Versailles, can still be reached by boat from Westminster, the usual means of travel in the days when it was a royal residence. Though very large, the palace has little of the Baroque grandeur of Versailles, but it is a fine example of two rewarding periods of English domestic architecture, the early 16th and the late 17th centuries.

The first builder of Hampton Court was Cardinal Wolsey, a man of humble birth who made the grave mistake of rivalling the monarch in magnificence. In 1529, as Wolsey's star declined, he presented the palace to Henry VIII in a vain effort to win back the King's favour. Henry enlarged it, making it probably the most luxurious palace in the country.

It is the Tudor palace, with its characteristic forest of extravagant chimneys, that you see on approaching through what is now the main entrance. Consisting basically of two courtyards with buildings on all sides, it bears a strong resemblance to the plan of the old colleges of Oxford and Cambridge. Built in red brick with towered gateways, it is fairly faithful to the English Gothic tradition, though Italian Renaissance influence can be seen, for example, in the terracotta roundels of Classical heads set in the walls. The palace, with a third court, later demolished, was regularly used by English monarchs during the 16th and 17th centuries.

During the reign of William and Mary (1689–1702) it was greatly enlarged. Sir Christopher Wren, England's most famous architect, was commissioned to build a new palace and, if his original plans had been fulfilled, all the Tudor buildings bar the Great Hall would have been swept away. As it is, Wren's coolly Classical Fountain Court and garden façade, in red brick with decorative use of Portland stone for colonnades, windows and balustrades, complement the more rugged Tudor courts. No monarch has resided there since George II.

Hampton Court has 'something for everyone', even young children, who can be safely left to explore the Maze (planted in the reign of Queen Anne). The most striking buildings are the early Tudor Chapel Royal, with an extraordinary vaulted ceiling that looks like stone but is actually wood; the Great Hall, with its rich hammerbeam roof; the recently restored kitchens, capable of providing a banquet for 500 people; the closed tennis court, much altered since Henry VIII played there; and the pleasant little Banquet Hall.

The treasures of the gardens include a Tudor knot garden, a magnificent screen of wrought-iron gates by Jean Tijou (late 17th century), and the great vine, planted in 1769 and still bearing grapes.

The Chapel Royal, Hampton Court, of which the most notable feature is the fan-vaulted wooden ceiling of Henry VIII's time.

Holyroodhouse

Holyroodhouse in Edinburgh is probably best known for its associations with that romantic royal heroine, Mary Queen of Scots. This is odd in that very little of the palace as it was in her time remains, and there are doubts whether the brass plate in the floor really marks the spot where Mary's secretary, David Rizzio, was bloodily murdered before her eyes by her husband's men. Soon afterwards her husband, Lord Darnley, was blown up by a bomb and Mary then married Lord Bothwell, a man of some notoriety, widely suspected of Darnley's murder. Mystery still surrounds these scandalous events, and seems to hang heavy over Holyrood.

The castle, a mixture of Scottish baronial, Italian Renaissance and domestic Baroque, was rebuilt a century after Mary's death to mark the restoration of the monarchy in 1660. The architect, Sir William Bruce, who had himself played a minor role in the events leading up to

Above: Vanbrugh, known to London society merely as a successful playwright, annoyed some people by his versatility. The news that he had been appointed to build Castle Howard was greeted sourly by Dean Swift:
Van's genius, without thought or lecture,
Is hugely turned to architecture.

Above left: At the palace of Holyroodhouse the shadow of Mary Queen of Scots is hard to escape. The severe Protestants of Edinburgh were shocked when they heard Mass had been celebrated within, and that carved heads of saints – even an organ – had been installed in the chapel.

Left: The Morning Drawing Room at Holyroodhouse was refurbished, along with the other state apartments, during the reign of George V and contains a suite of chairs covered in tapestry worked by Scottish ladies and presented to Queen Mary in the 1920s.

the Restoration, was taken by the large tower which remained from the time of that most attractive of Scottish monarchs, James IV (1488–1513). He added a similar structure at the other end of the building, with a Classical entrance portico surmounted by a stone lantern. Much of the interior decoration, which includes particularly fine plasterwork, was by Flemish and Dutch craftsmen. The palace had originated as a lodging house attached to the medieval abbey of Holyrood, and the ruined abbey church still adjoins the 17th-century palace.

The palace is a very handsome, beautifully situated building, and inside the scale is comparatively modest (for that reason, it is rather more comfortable than many royal palaces). It has played a minor role since Scotland was united with England in 1707, occasionally inhabited by royal refugees such as the Comte d'Artois (Charles X), and it was rather dilapidated until restored in the 1820s at the instigation of George IV. It is still used by the monarch when visiting the Scottish capital.

Castle Howard

Various branches of the Howard family have figured prominently in English history since the 15th century. Their principal home, not far from York, is possibly the most spectacularly beautiful country house in England. It has recently become familiar to millions who have never visited it by being cast in the title role in the television film (1981) of Evelyn Waugh's novel, *Brideshead Revisited*.

It was commissioned by Charles Howard, 3rd Earl of Carlisle, in 1699 and built on the site of an old castle to the design of Sir John Vanbrugh, who was assisted, here as at Blenheim Palace a few years later, by Nicholas Hawksmoor. Although incomplete when Vanbrugh died in 1726, the house was finished by Sir Thomas Robinson in 1759.

This was Vanbrugh's first commission. He had no training as an architect and Castle Howard has been called by a contemporary critic 'an amazing trial of strength by a young undisciplined genius'. Vanbrugh's style owed something, clearly, to Wren, though it was grander and more ostentatious, and something (no one is sure how much) to Hawksmoor.

The main southern façade consists of a central block, seeming higher than it is owing to the fluted Classical pilasters and the slender gilded dome which rises amid a host of statuary behind the central pediment, with low wings on either side. Inside, the Great Hall rises to the full height of the building, from floor to lantern. The other outstanding room is the graceful Long Gallery, containing paintings by Holbein, Van Dyck, Lely and other masters. There is some fine furniture, and in the Stable Court a permanent exhibition of historic costume.

The palace enjoys a superb setting, and the grounds contain, besides lakes, fountain and gardens, Vanbrugh's beautiful little Temple of the Four Winds and Hawksmoor's circular, colonnaded mausoleum.

Kensington Palace

The 19th-century writer Leigh Hunt remarked of the royal palaces in London that 'Windsor Castle is a place to receive monarchs in; Buckingham Palace to see fashion in; Kensington Palace seems a place to drink tea in . . .' It is one of those royal residences which, from modest beginnings, was extended, altered and enlarged through the generations like a termites' nest and has ended up an attractive jumble.

William III took a dislike to the palace of Whitehall, chiefly because its riverside site had a bad effect on his asthma. Hampton Court, though

Castle Howard's main entrance hall, below the dome, is 11 metres (12 yards) square. Contemporaries thought it ponderous and overweight. Perhaps the girl with the broom is intended to add a lightening touch.

more attractive, was also close to the river and too far out for convenience. After a little house hunting, he settled on Nottingham House, an unpretentious Jacobean villa. It was far too small for the royal court and Sir Christopher Wren was employed to make extensions. The court moved in for Christmas 1689.

Wren's work has suffered from later alterations. His finest room, the King's Gallery, is 30 metres (66 feet) long with a grand panelled ceiling added by William Kent in 1727 and a curious device which, connected with a weather vane on the roof, enables those within to tell the direction of the wind.

The palace was occupied by British monarchs from William and Mary to George II. Queen Anne added the stately Orangery, by Wren and Sir John Vanbrugh, and laid out Kensington Gardens. Extensive reconstruction took place for George I: the original core of Nottingham House was demolished and replaced by the magnificent Cupola Room, by Vanbrugh and Kent. The Round Pond and what is now the Serpentine were constructed in the gardens along with the Queen's Temple, a summerhouse now serving as a keeper's lodge, and a (vanished) arbour which revolved to face away from the wind.

'My earliest recollections are connected with Kensington Palace', wrote Queen Victoria in her fifties, '... I can remember crawling on a yellow carpet spread out for that purpose ...' But her childhood in this genial setting was 'rather melancholy'.

Palaces of France

Château d'Anet

Though much of it has disappeared, the Château d'Anet is still one of the most remarkable royal, or semi-royal, palaces in France. Henri II had it built for his mistress Diane de Poitiers between 1547 and 1552 by the most gifted French architect of the period, Philibert Delorme. Delorme had a profound grasp of the fundamentals of Italian Renaissance architecture, and also a daring impulse to experiment. He is said to have expressed a desire to build a mansion that was neither a traditional French château nor a traditional Italian palazzo.

The result was an extraordinary building, a riotous assembly of cubes and curves, with many quite novel features, including an emphasis on texture (by skilful mixture of brick, stone and black marble); a domed chapel (the first in France) of remarkable geometric subtlety, with sculptures attributed to Jean Goujon, and a fantastic entrance gate deriving from the Roman triumphal arch, with elaborate pierced balconies from which the ladies watched the hunting parties setting off for the forest of Dreux. Bernini's bronze relief of Diana, goddess of the chase (a frequent allusion at Anet) has been replaced by a replica.

The general effect of Philibert Delorme's masterpiece was at the same time monumental yet playful. However, the surviving parts of the building (only one wing of the main structure remains) have been much altered. As you stand in the main hall, before the cascading staircase between fantasized Roman figures holding lamps, you are looking at 17th-century work, carried out after the château became the property of the duc de Vendôme. It arouses the mixed feelings that are inevitably provoked by contemplation of one masterpiece created at the expense of another. The gardens were re-landscaped by André le Nôtre, responsible also for Versailles among other famous ornamental gardens, and some of his parterres and galleries have also disappeared. Although it is now difficult to envisage fully Philibert Delorme's original creation (the entrance arch

Above: The figure of Diana reclines in the tympanum over a fine pair of wooden doors at the Château d'Anet.

Far right: A view of Philibert de l'Orme's (Delorme's) fascinating hunting lodge from beyond the moat.

Right: Intriguing figures holding lamps in the hall at the Château d'Anet. They date from the Louis XIV period, and one cannot help thinking that Caesar would never have conquered Gaul with these epicene warriors.

The Papal Palace at Avignon has a fortress-like appearance which, rightly or wrongly, seems to echo the theme of 'Babylonian Captivity', that rather shabby period in the history of the papacy.

of the main building can be seen, re-erected, in the Ecôle des Beaux-Arts in Paris), the Château d'Anet still attracts many visitors. No doubt the seductive powers of its first, extra-ordinary chatelaine are still at work.

Palace of the Popes, Avignon

In 1305 Bertrand de Gouth, arch-bishop of Bordeaux, was elected pope as Clement V despite being neither a cardinal nor an Italian. One of his first acts was to create a number of French cardinals. He delayed going to Rome, and eventually settled down with the whole papal court at Avignon in 1309. This was the beginning of the 'Babylonian Captivity' – of absentee popes under French control – and of the decline of papal authority in Europe. It was not until 1377 that Pope Gregory XI returned to Rome, and on his death in the following year two rival popes were elected, one in Rome and the other at Avignon. The 'Great Schism' continued, with three popes in the field at one time, until 1417.

Avignon has, therefore, a unique role in the history of the Roman Catholic Church, and the Papal

Palace stands as a monument to the near-failure of the papacy in medieval Christendom. It is a rather severe assembly of Gothic buildings; its great cliff-like walls make it look more like a fortress than a palace, and the almost total absence of furniture adds a sombre note to the already rather gloomy interior. The palace does, however, form a splendid back-ground to the international festival now held at Avignon every year.

The palace dates mainly from the 14th and early 15th centuries and, as the former citadel of the papal state of Avignon, it is a huge complex, with numerous public chambers, chapels, courtyards, towers and gardens. It has suffered a good deal of damage in modern times, like the famous pont d'Avignon (with its little Romanesque chapel) which still sets out boldly over the Rhône but has not, for many years, reached the other bank. Partly looted during the French Revolution, the palace became a barracks for Napoleon's troops, who are said to have taken everything that could be moved for sale to the local citizens. Although they allegedly went so far as to hack

off sections of frescoed wall, they missed the remarkable work in the Oratory of St Michael painted by followers of Duccio of Siena.

Château de Balleroy

François Mansart (1598–1666) was one of the first and most gifted architects in the tradition of French classicism, and the Château de Balleroy in Normandy is one of his earliest works, planned when he was only 28 years old. The building is really a country house, though a very grand one, with some attributes of a medieval castle, notably a large moat (never filled) and little outlying turrets which would never have been

the slightest use in defence against attack. It survived the wreckers of the Revolutionary period thanks to a skilfully engineered rumour in the village of infectious disease within, and it survived the Allied attack on Normandy in 1944 because it was then serving as a hospital In fact the appearance today of the château, seen from the front, is precisely the same as Mansart's design of 1626. After 350 years this is remarkable enough, but particularly so because of the architect's notorious tendency to change his own plans in the course of construction.

The château follows the basic Classical plan of a large central block

Sound rings hollow today in the great empty chambers of the Palace of the Popes, and it is easy to imagine shadowy figures in dark corners.

with wings on either side, but otherwise it is distinctly unconventional and signified the emergence of a daring and individual genius. Immediately striking is the great height of the three elements in relation to their width. The very tall windows of the first and second storeys in fact created problems inside, as the floor levels of the smaller rooms do not match them. This is the most obvious fault in Mansart's design – though the Salon d'Honneur, with fine royal portraits, is a magnificent chamber.

From these steep roofs with their elegantly arched dormer windows you can, with the advantage of hindsight, visualize the development of the Mansard roof, named after its originator. The roof of the main block rises to a low gallery around the rectangular space on which rests, perhaps a trifle uneasily, a slender cupola.

After the general shape of the structure, the most remarkable feature is the actual fabric. The walls appear to be brick, but are actually of a rusty grey stone, cut to the approximate size of bricks, and the windows and corners are ornamented with quoins of dressed Caen stone. There is no other exterior ornament – not a scroll or an acanthus leaf or a putto's head in sight. In front are parterres and ornamental flower gardens in the French style, and there is a magnificent approach to the building – down the village street then continuing in a straight line up the long slope of the carriageway – which greatly enhances the restrained grandeur of the château.

Its striking verticality is perhaps the most immediately apparent feature of the Château de Balleroy's exterior.

Right: The main courtyard of the Château de Blois with the famous staircase in its octagonal open tower on the right.

Château de Blois

In many ways the Château de Blois can be regarded as the typical Loire château. Substantial remnants of the medieval castle can still be seen, along with elements from the Renaissance and later periods.

Blois was a place of some importance in the early Middle Ages though the earliest medieval remains date only from the 13th century. They include the Great Hall, where the States General met during the reign of Louis XIII and, at the opposite end of the château, the Tour de Foix, which commands a splendid view over the terrace.

During the 15th century the castle was the favourite residence of Charles d'Orléans, most notable of royal poets who, having been captured at Agincourt, spent half his adult life in captivity in England. He pulled down part of the old fortress in favour of more comfortable accommodation, but nothing much of his château remains except the truncated gallery adjoining the east wing. The latter, now a museum and art gallery, belongs to the reign of Louis XII, who also carried out extensive renovations. The gallery along the façade, linking the rooms, was a fairly novel idea in 1500; previously one room could only be entered from the next.

The buildings are grouped around a courtyard, and the largest elements today are the early 16th-century wing of François I and, on the west, the E-shaped block built in the 17th century by François Mansart for Gaston d'Orléans. The former was begun little more than a decade after the Louis XII wing was completed, but marked changes are evident, reflecting the influence of the Italian Renaissance. The most famous feature is the exterior staircase, ascending in a projecting octagonal tower rich with sculpture, the balustrade slashing bold diagonals across the façade. Originally, it formed the centrepiece of the façade from the courtyard, but it is no longer in the middle, since Mansart made free with earlier structures when erecting his palatial addition in the Classical style during the 1630s. Mansart's plans were not completed (presumably because Cardinal Richelieu cut off Gaston d'Orléans's subsidy once he had ceased to be a political threat). If they had been, he would no doubt have created a

An equestrian statue of Louis XII over the entrance gate at Blois. A disastrous treaty with the Emperor was signed at the château during Louis's reign, presaging the long and violent rivalry of the French monarchy and the Habsburgs.

building grander than the Luxembourg palace. As it is, Mansart's building is a masterpiece, and displays the first example of the type of double-sloped roof known, after him, as a Mansard roof.

The Château de Blois hoards more than an average number of secrets and scandals. Guides point out, accurately or not, the window from which the portly Marie de Medicis was lowered by a rope (thus escaping the captivity imposed by her son, Louis XII), and indicate the secret cupboards, opened by a lever, in the chamber of Catherine de Medicis. But the most sensational event was the assassination of the duc de Guise on the orders of Henri III in 1588. The powerful duke is said to have thrown off four of his eight assailants before he fell at the foot of the King's bed. 'My God,' Henri exclaimed, 'he looks even bigger dead than alive.'

Chambord

Approached from the north-west at sunset, the château of Chambord, largest and most famous of the châteaux of the Loire, appears out of the forest like a castle in a fairytale, a vision of pale stone surmounted by a lively crowd of decorative towers, turrets and chimneys, casting a shimmering reflection on the river flowing by.

Unlike its neighbour at Blois, Chambord is architecturally uniform. François I devoted enormous resources to its construction and, despite interruptions, it was virtually finished before his death in 1547. Subsequent alterations were minor, and Chambord remains perhaps the outstanding building of the early Renaissance in France. Despite the Italian influence, the basic plan is similar to that of a medieval castle – a rectangle (approximately 160 by 120 metres) around a courtyard with a main block, equivalent to the medieval keep, at the centre of the north-west façade. There are large round towers at each corner of the main building and at the ends of the main façade. The moat, filled by diversion of the River Cosson (François wanted to divert the Loire itself, but his engineers boggled), was liable to flooding and was filled in during the 18th century. The immense, wooded deer park, surrounded by a wall over 30 km long, still remains. Park and château are now the property of the French republic.

The chief designer of Chambord was an Italian, Domenico da Cortona, but the successive masters of the works were French masons, who greatly influenced the final result – an intriguing mixture of Renaissance and Gothic features. The most famous feature of the château is the central staircase, ascending through four storeys at the point where four lofty, barrel-vaulted halls meet. It is a double spiral, so that someone coming down never passes someone going up, and as it is contained only by slim, square columns, there is a view of the whole of each floor from the staircase.

Although one or two rooms have recently been restored to an earlier – if not the original – state, the furnishings disappeared during the Revolutionary period, and despite all the decorative details the interior now looks rather bare.

Louis XIV visited Chambord on several occasions, and saw there the first performances of two of Molière's plays. Louis XV gave the château to Stanislas Leczinski after he had been thrown out of Poland, and later to Maurice de Saxe, following the Marshal's famous victory over the Duke of Cumberland at Fontenoy (1745). His troops, including Tartars from the Asian steppes and blacks from Martinique, were allowed the freedom of the park, acts of indiscipline being punished by summary hangings from elm trees.

Chantilly

Chantilly, like its owners, the Condés, had a chequered history. Now one of the most impressive museums in France, it belongs in fact very largely to the 19th century, though the rebuilding of that period

A lonely little French princess used to play hide-and-seek on *le grand escalier* – the extraordinary double staircase which is the central feature of the Château de Chambord.

The Prince de Condé's study at Chantilly. The furniture is, of course, set out for the convenience of sightseers (and the photographer), who are not encouraged to wander about too freely.

followed, fairly closely, the 17th-century reconstruction by Mansart.

'The king arrived in Chantilly last night,' wrote the diarist Mme de Sévigné in 1676. 'He hunted a stag by moonlight. The lanterns worked wonders [but] the fireworks were rather dim, outshone by the light of our friend the moon. Anyway, the evening, the supper, the gaming, were all splendid.' The enjoyment of the company was nonetheless sullied by the suicide of the steward who, in the best traditions of French *haute cuisine*, stabbed himself to death when he was informed – incorrectly as it happened – that the fish had failed to arrive on time. Louis XIV, not quite such an inhuman figure as he is sometimes portrayed, was thoroughly upset, and begged for less lavish entertainment in future.

That sad incident is symptomatic of the fortunes of Chantilly and its owners for much of its existence, the Montmorencys and the Bourbon princes of Condé. The court of the *Grand Condé* at the time of Louis XIV's visit was nearly as splendid as Versailles and possibly more interesting, as it attracted the most brilliant writers of the day.

The medieval castle was reconstructed in the 16th century by Anne de Montmorency, constable of France (he was named after his godmother), who also built a smaller *châtelet* nearby. The latter survives, though the main château was completely rebuilt by Mansart. The gardens were laid out by André le Nôtre, and included a menagerie.

The Condés were among the first refugees from the French Revolution, which wrought fearful havoc at Chantilly. The main building was completely destroyed (as was Le Nôtre's landscape) but rebuilt about 1880 to Mansart's plans. On the death of the duc d'Aumale (son of Louis-Philippe) the whole property passed into the possession of the Institut de France.

Chantilly is, of course, famous for horse racing, and the 18th-century stables must be among the most splendid accommodation for animals in Europe. When the Tsar dined in this building he thought, not knowing the layout, that he was in the grandest chamber of the palace. The contents of Chantilly today are largely due to the duc d'Aumale, a keen collector not only of paintings (Poussin, Clouet, etc) but also of manuscripts, sculpture and tapestries. The ponds, glades and trees still form a magnificent setting, and lovers may still wander, under the benign gaze of a marble Cupid, in the 'English' garden on the Ile d'Amour.

Châteaudun

Châteaudun lies about midway between Chartres and Orléans, on a tributary of the Loire called, confusingly, the Loir. The town is dominated by the château, perched on a rocky outcrop. Originally a fortress of the counts of Dunois, it was turned into a palace by Louis of Orléans, son of Charles V, about the end of the 14th century.

It is still essentially a Gothic castle, with its great round donjon (keep), its cliff-like walls, and its delicate, late 15th-century chapel, with beautiful statues of saints, built by that romantic figure, Jean Dunois, the Bastard of Orléans, who in alliance with Joan of Arc drove the English out of France. He also built the wing adjoining the chapel and keep, its light and spacious rooms lit by tall windows. Extensive rebuilding was planned by the Bastard's grandson, but except for the long north wing, itself incomplete, the plans were never carried out. The north wing is again basically Gothic, with giant oak beams and wooden shutters carved in the pattern known (for obvious reasons) as linenfold, though the influence of the Renaissance is evident in some decorative details.

The most striking feature of Châteaudun is the famous circular staircase which, unlike most later staircases of this kind, is integrated into the building, with direct access to galleries on each floor. It is a

Above: Tranquil saints and arrow-like forms — the culmination of the Gothic style in France as seen in the chapel at Châteaudun.

The buildings at Châteaudun are grouped around a rugged circular donjon, or keep, the stronghold of a medieval castle.

perfect example of the culminating style of French Gothic known as Flamboyant, an appropriate name, as the flame-like forms (almost suggesting Art Nouveau design) of the mullioned windows testify.

Fontainebleau

Fontainebleau is one of the oldest royal châteaux built by François I, and it set the style for much of the architecture and decorative art in France during the 16th century, as is evident from a tour of the châteaux of the Loire. There was a medieval castle here, though what remains of it is largely 16th-century reconstruction. Different elements were added at different times under François I and his successors down to Napoleon, and there was never a recognizable plan. Parts of the Renaissance structure were lost during 18th-century rebuilding and 19th-century 'restoration'.

Set amid a beautiful forest (excellent hunting in former times), the palace with its park and gardens occupies an enormous site. From across the carp pond (whose inhabitants in the 19th century were believed to be the original fish placed there by François I) you can see buildings erected over the course of

three centuries. Thanks partly to the use of the same reddish sandstone, there is no sense of incongruity and, in any case, what Fontainebleau lacks in architectural cohesion it more than makes up for in decorative splendour. It is the decorative features of the Renaissance palace which are its chief glory.

The old core of the palace is the Oval Courtyard, where a medieval tower is one of an attractive mishmash of buildings in a colonnaded crescent. The Gallery of François I links them with the newer buildings around the White Horse Courtyard, on the south side of which once stood the famous Gallery of Ulysses, demolished, unfortunately, in the 18th century to make way for the Neo-Classical Louis XV wing.

The Gallery of François I was built in 1531 and decorated during the ensuing decade by the Florentine artist, Il Roso ('Maître Rous'), who may be regarded as the founder of the School of Fontainebleau. The decoration consists of a mixture of wood, plaster and frescoes. The lower part of the walls (65 metres (215 feet) long) is panelled in carved and partly gilded walnut. Above, the paintings of scenes from Classical mythology are richly framed with stucco (carved

Fontainebleau has been called 'the result of a chance meeting of a group of châteaux'. It is a vast, rambling place in which a host of separate wings have accumulated around five courtyards.

35

Above: The Gallery of François I, which set the style of delicate Mannerism in French art named after the palace at Fontainebleau.

The ballroom at Fontainebleau, decorated by Primaticcio, dates from the reign of Henri II (1547–59), when painting was becoming dominant over stucco.

plasterwork). The integrated composition is a masterpiece, unparalleled if not unique in its time, and sets the style characteristic of Fontainebleau.

Rosso was succeeded in 1541 by a possibly greater artist, Primaticcio of Bologna. His masterpiece was the Gallery of Ulysses, now known only from tapestries and inadequate engravings, but fortunately much of his work does survive, notably on the King's Staircase and in the bedchamber of the duchesse d'Etampes (mistress of François I). It is here that we find those stucco figures which are perhaps the most familiar products of the first School of Fontainebleau, the elegant female nudes, of Gothic slimness and Classical pose. These coolly erotic figures frame frescoes illustrating scenes from the life of Alexander the Great (perhaps an odd choice for a lady's bedroom). The splendid ballroom was also decorated by Primaticcio together with the third outstanding Italian artist employed at Fontainebleau, Niccolo dell' Abbate, while the elaborate wooden ceiling (another characteristic of Fontainebleau) was probably designed by the brilliant French architect, Philibert Delorme, who also designed the original Horseshoe

Staircase (later altered, and not horseshoe-shaped any longer).

Fontainebleau, the scene of many sensational historical incidents, became the favourite imperial residence of Napoleon – hence the Empire-style furniture in Rococo apartments. The room where Pope Pius VII was held prisoner for two years can be seen more or less as it was then, and the Fountain Court has not changed since Napoleon took his affecting farewell from his troops there, before setting off for exile on the island of Elba. Later, the palace was used again as a royal residence by Louis-Philippe and briefly as a presidential palace under the Republic.

The Louvre
As everyone knows, the Louvre is one of the greatest museums and art galleries in the world. But not everyone who gazes at the Mona Lisa or the Venus de Milo realizes that it was once a royal palace and, before the building of Versailles, the chief residence of the French court.

There was a fort on the site in the reign of Louis VI (1108–37), but as the city expanded beyond its early defences the fort gradually changed into a palace. In the 16th century François I, urged by the Parisians to

The Louvre is not only (as every visitor to Paris knows) a treasure house of world art, but also of French architecture, incorporating aspects from nearly every period from the Middle Ages to the 19th century.

spend more time in their midst (to the advantage of trade), agreed to build a fine palace there, but construction did not begin until shortly before his death. However, work continued: Pierre Lescot's Classical buildings, with sculpture by Jean Goujon, arose around a square (much smaller than the present one), and although the palace was so much enlarged in later times, Lescot and Goujon set the style for later additions.

When the widowed Catherine de Médicis came to the Louvre about 1560, she decided she needed larger quarters and commissioned the building of the Tuileries palace (destroyed in 1871) to the west. Henri IV completed the gallery on the river front and carried forward Catherine's plan to link the Louvre with the Tuileries. The last monarch to reside there for any time, he also turned the ground floor into a museum and school of craftsmanship. Under Louis XIII the main quadrangle was enlarged to its present size by Jacques le Mercier, who pulled down two wings of the old château but remained generally loyal to Lescot's conception. The royal mint and the royal printing house moved in. The palace continued to grow, in the hands of Louis Le Vau, despite Louis XIV's preoccupation with Versailles; the most notable addition was the eastern colonnade by Claude Perrault, a delightful and original structure.

Little more was done until the time of Napoleon, when the north wing was added, finally completing the link with the Tuileries. The 'Nouveau Louvre', north and south of the Place Napoléon III, was erected in the 1850s.

It would be impossible to summarize the treasures of the Louvre in a sentence or two. Apart from the collections of antiquities, drawings and objets d'art, the paintings are probably what the average visitor first wishes to see. François I was the first great royal collector, and the Italian Renaissance masterpieces are due to him. Many of his successors added richly to the royal collection, not least Napoleon, who extracted works of art from conquered countries – not

There seems to be some form of chemistry which governs people's feelings for places. The Luxembourg Gardens evoke an affection among Parisians that the palace itself fails to arouse.

One of the grand saloons in Marie de Médicis's palace, which her unsuccessful political intrigues prevented her living in for long.

all of which were returned after 1815. The Louvre, having narrowly avoided destruction during the Revolutionary period, was turned into a museum instead, and it then acquired many treasures from less fortunate French palaces.

Luxembourg Palace

The handsome Luxembourg palace, adjoining the Boulevard St Michel in Paris, is the work of Salomon de Brosse (1571–1626), perhaps the finest French architect of his generation if not of the whole century. Though it was enlarged and altered in the 19th century, it remains the finest example of late Renaissance architecture in Paris still surviving; the addition of another storey to the north façade has done less damage to the proportions than might have been expected. The south façade was completely rebuilt, but in the original style.

The Luxembourg palace really ought to be called the Medici palace, as it was built for Marie de Medicis, wife of Henri IV and later queen mother and regent, but so heartily did the Parisians dislike her that they insisted on calling it after the original owner, the duc de Luxembourg. Rather than move into the Tuileries, then under construction, the homesick, embittered widow decided in 1612 on a magnificent new residence, on the south bank, far from the city mobs, which would remind her of her home, the Pitti palace in Florence. De Brosse was originally ordered to design a copy of the Pitti, but the only resemblance the Luxembourg bears to it is the rusticated stonework of the lower walls.

When Louis XIII came of age, he executed his mother's favourites (always a popular move) and banished her to Blois, but in 1625 she returned to live, powerless, in the Luxembourg, until forced into exile by Cardinal Richelieu in 1631.

Today the palace is rather better known for its famous gardens, also designed originally by de Brosse, where students discuss radical politics and children play with boats in the pond.

Right: The Château de Maisons, later known as Maisons-Lafitte, is the finest, or most complete, masterpiece of François Mansart, and one of the most pleasantly harmonious châteaux in France.

Classical serenity and restrained opulence: the ballroom at Château Maisons-Lafitte.

Château Maisons-Lafitte

The Château Maisons-Lafitte, near Paris, is the most perfect surviving work of the great Classical architect François Mansart (see also the châteaux of Balleroy and Blois). Designed on a symmetrical E-plan with central entrance, it is notable for the effective way in which the Classical orders are combined with high roofs and chimneys, and, internally, for its elegant oval rooms in the pavilions and the main hall.

The château was built in the 1640s for René de Longueuil, who had amassed a vast fortune in the service of Cardinal Richelieu. He was a tolerant patron, apparently uttering no complaint when the perfectionist Mansart pulled down the half-completed building because he was not satisfied with its appearance. The château was formally inaugurated by the official visit of the Queen Mother, Anne of Austria, with the 13-year-old Louis XIV in tow, in 1651.

In the 18th century a fire did some damage, then shortly before the Revolution it was acquired by the flamboyant but stupid Comte d'Artois (later Charles X), who constructed the famous race course. Having survived the intervening years without serious damage, it was purchased after the Restoration by Jacques Lafitte, the influential banker and politician. After his fall from power in 1831 Lafitte, in dire need of cash, built a housing estate – one of the first 'garden suburbs' – in the park, knocking down Mansart's beautiful stables for building stone. In 1904 the château itself was saved from the same fate by the intervention of the state, and it was restored, as far as possible, to its original condition.

Malmaison

Malmaison is essentially a country house, a grand one certainly, which owes its fame chiefly to its romantic association with Napoleon Bonaparte and Josephine de Beauharnais. The original house was built in the 17th century, a comparatively simple building consisting of a three-storeyed central block with short protruding wings. Though looted during the Revolution, it escaped serious damage, and in 1799 Josephine bought it while Napoleon was in Egypt. It was later enlarged, and the rather unfortunate buttresses topped by vases had to be added to support a structure weakened by demolition of the original wings.

Josephine adored the house, which was her home for the rest of her life. For Napoleon it was a country retreat, 45 minutes on horseback from Paris, to which he repaired as often as state business permitted. At Malmaison, his intimates reported, Napoleon was at his most relaxed and amiable, abandoning consular dignity for games of blind man's bluff. It was there too that he spent his last days of freedom, after Waterloo. Josephine, divorced in 1809, had died there a year earlier.

Malmaison passed through many hands during the 19th century, and a large part of the park, of which Josephine was so fond (her greenhouses supplied botanical gardens all over France), disappeared. Its last private owner generously presented the château to the French nation in 1904 and it was opened as a museum soon afterwards. It is essentially a monument to the French Empire style, and although most of the

In the grounds of Malmaison, one may still smell the fragrance of the Empress Josephine's roses. 'Malmaison is only a sigh', wrote a French poet, '. . . a place of great languor, an urn for the ashes of the heart . . .'

The circular tent-like bedchamber of the Empress Josephine, whose initial is embroidered on the furniture and whose portrait hangs on the wall.

Far right: The library at Malmaison: the cold and pompous Empire-style furniture does not accurately reflect the spirit of the place.

pictures which hung there in Napoleon's time are now in the Hermitage in Leningrad (bought by the Tsar to ease the financial plight of Josephine's son, Eugène), the Empress's circular bedroom, with crimson drapes hung between gilt columns, the dining room panelled with statuesque nymphs in grisaille, the library and other rooms are much as they were in the Emperor's time. The presence of Josephine is perhaps most closely felt in the rose garden, or standing under the spreading cedar, planted by her to mark the victory of Marengo in 1800.

Château Rambouillet

The great age of royal palace-building in France was the 17th century, before the clouds, in the shape of grievous financial shortages, began to shade the Sun King, Louis XIV, in the later part of his reign. Eighteenth-century palaces were smaller and less solemn in purpose: typically, they were elegant residences, like Mme de Pompadour's Bellevue, designed for a royal mistress. Besides these two categories – the grand Baroque palaces and the royal Rococo mansions of the age of Louis XV – there was a third type of royal château, of which Rambouillet is one example. Generally these are much older, often bearing signs of their medieval role as a fortress but surviving into the gunpowder age to be transformed into a hunting lodge or rural residence.

The first château, a simple forti-fied house, was built in the 14th century. It changed hands more than once in the course of the Hundred Years' War. The major survival from that time is the tower named after François I, who is said to have died there after being taken ill while hunting nearby. Renaissance additions included a ground-floor gallery and the creation of extensive gardens, with orderly canals to drain the former swamp. Soon afterwards the property passed into the hands of the comte de Toulouse, a son of Louis XIV, who enlarged it considerably, retaining most of the medieval walls but adding Classical façades. Some of the intricately carved woodwork, which dates from this time, is especially notable.

In 1784 the château came into the possession of Louis XVI. It appears that, as happened with many another desirable residence, he merely expressed a liking for it and the proprietor took the hint. The King wanted it for a hunting lodge; Marie Antoinette, his queen consort, was allegedly less keen on the place, and some alterations were made for her convenience.

The Revolution saved Rambouillet from more extensive rebuilding, and eventually it was restored by Napoleon, who also appreciated the hunting. He pulled down one wing, rebuilt the main gate and the east turret, and had his own suite of rooms next to the Tour François I.

In accordance with the priorities of an earlier age, the bath is the least impressive article in the imperial bathroom at Rambouillet.

The garden façade at Rambouillet. The château has an ancient history, and changed hands three times during the Anglo-French wars of the later Middle Ages.

St Germain-en-Laye

The present château of St Germain, though imposing, represents only part of what was once an enormous complex. The Château Neuf, which old engravings show to have been a gigantic barracks of a place with an artful arrangement of exterior staircases giving access to four very tall storeys, disappeared during the Revolution. The Château Vieux, though neglected for many years, has now been restored as a museum. The superb terrace, over 2 km long, commanding a view over the Seine to Paris and rejoicing in the reputation of 'the finest promenade in Europe', remains as it was in the late 17th century.

The original castle, built by Louis VI early in the 12th century, was destroyed by the English and rebuilt on several subsequent occasions; its existence as a royal palace really dates from the time of François I. The most notable survival from medieval times is the early 13th-century chapel of St Louis, possibly by the builder of the Sainte-Chapelle in Paris; it is also quite gem-like.

Left: In the 18th century the Comte de Toulouse was responsible for this remarkable woodwork at Rambouillet, in which oak takes on an almost lace-like delicacy.

St Germain was neglected by the early Valois kings but engaged the interest of François, perhaps because he had been married there. He appointed Pierre Chambiges to organize the alterations, and although much of the work was completed after that architect's death in 1544, the building is in the early French Renaissance style that Chambiges represented. Perhaps its most remarkable feature is the terraced roof of great stone slabs, which had to be supported by large stone buttresses reinforced with iron.

The balustrade that runs along the edge of the roof has slender stone vases at intervals, above the buttresses, and this feature is reproduced in the gallery at second-storey level. The effect is harmonious. The plan follows the outline of the earlier castle and incorporates a 14th-century tower at the north-west corner. During the next hundred years or so a number of additions were made. Many of the architectural giants of the 17th century worked here, and the great Le Nôtre planned the terrace.

Many famous French architects worked at Saint Germain but, fundamentally, the early 16th-century designs of Chambiges were followed. The originality and harmony of his style suffered slightly from the need to follow the military aspect of the earlier castle.

Versailles is saved from appearing too heavy and ponderous by the rich array of statuary on the cornice which, thanks to the flatness of the roof, breaks up the outline.

While Versailles was being built, St Germain was Louis XIV's favourite residence, and no doubt the duc de Saint Simon was not alone in deploring the move to Versailles in 1682. St Germain thereupon became redundant, but it proved useful when James II of England fled to France in 1688. For many years the exiled Stuarts held unhappy court there, living on hope, French promises and French brandy. Napoleon III decided to renovate it as a museum of antiquities. The exterior was properly restored, but the interior had to be almost totally reconstructed in accordance with its new role.

Versailles

Siamese ambassadors to the court of King Louis XIV were stunned by the sheer size of the place. Many eminent visitors of later times, not forgetting the footsore sightseers, have experienced similar sensations. Versailles, the grandest royal palace in Europe, is really much too large to see in a day's trip from nearby Paris; a week would not be too much. In the late 17th and 18th centuries it was capable of holding practically the entire ruling class of France – and, indeed, frequently did.

Versailles was begun virtually from nothing, yet although most of the early building was completed quite fast, the whole complex is more of a hotch-potch than it first appears. The first royal building on the site was a small hunting lodge (a mere twenty rooms or so) belonging to Louis XIII. A more retiring monarch than his successor, Louis XIII grew to like the place, bought up the land round about, and created a park and a château.

In the 1660s, Louis XIV decided to enlarge it. He was not particularly pleased with his other chief residences, least of all the Louvre, where his minister Colbert thought the court should reside, and at the same time he felt an urge to symbolize his own eminence (or the eminence of France – the same thing, so far as Louis was concerned) by creating a new citadel.

The man whom Louis chose to plan a new setting for his palace was André le Nôtre, the most famous of French landscape designers. He laid out the 'gardens of intelligence' in the formal manner dearer to the logical French than the romantic English, the great canal and the Grand Parc. The waspish duc de Saint Simon's complaint that the land was swampy yet waterless was not unjustified, and enormous engineering works were projected, including the diversion of the River Eure (subsequently abandoned), to drain the site and to supply over a thousand fountains. The latter, however, were turned off as soon as the King departed; there are about 600 in action today. The gardens were liberally sprinkled with sculpture under the direction of Charles le Brun; Apollo's chariot of the sun rises from one of the pools.

The building was the responsibility of Louis Le Vau, who incorporated the old château, and opted for terraced roofs, breaking up the stark horizontals of the cornice with grand sculpture. Le Vau died in the 1670s and was eventually replaced by Jules Hardouin-Mansart who, of all the famous names associated with the building of Versailles, contributed most to the final building. He vastly extended Le Vau's palace to the north and south, created the famous Hall of Mirrors, and built the royal chapel, decorated by Antoine Coypel and a team of artists following the directions of Louis himself.

Life at Versailles revolved around the person of the King: every little incident of his daily life was the subject of intricate ritual. Ceremony prevented him eating a hot meal or changing his own shirt, and Louis moved among a constant throng, not only of courtiers but of petitioners and sightseers, in fact anyone who could afford to hire a sword from the gatekeepers – a condition of admission, like neckties at smart restaurants. But even at Versailles, Louis could sometimes escape the crowds, retiring to the Grand Trianon, a pavilion on the site of a village of that name, where he gave little parties for his favourites.

The last years of the reign, when the King was old and his resources drained by his frequent wars, were gloomy, but Versailles took on a new lease of life under Louis XV, whose name is associated with the French Rococo style in art and decoration, so much lighter and more consciously graceful than the heavy, ceremonial Baroque of Louis XIV. The furniture became more elegant and more comfortable, and though some of the architectural additions marred the harmony of the scheme of Le Vau and Hardouin-Mansart, Jacques-Ange Gabriel created the luxurious opera house, as well as the little Classical villa of the Petit Trianon, which became the favourite resi-

dence of Marie Antoinette. There was a little farm where she could pretend to be a milkmaid, a romantic 'English' garden and a superb little temple of love, with a statue of Cupid by Bouchardon.

Retribution for all this expensive display came in 1789, when the Paris mob marched on Versailles. The King and Queen were doomed, but although looters ransacked the palace and the pools later silted up, Versailles suffered remarkably little during the Revolutionary period. Louis-Philippe turned it into a museum, filling it with rather boring academic paintings of historical events. Serious restoration began in the 20th century and is still continuing. Today, much of the glory of Versailles in the days of Louis XV and the lovable Mme de Pompadour has returned, and the palace is, as the Sun King intended it to be, an illustrious memorial to the greatness of the French monarchy.

Overleaf: The famous Galerie des Glaces, or Hall of Mirrors, at Versailles. The paintings on the ceiling depict scenes from the life of Louis XIV, and the whole ensemble provides an unsurpassable setting for royal ceremonial of the most lavish kind.

The light and airy royal chapel at Versailles, the work of Hardouin-Mansart, was consecrated in 1710. The painting of the Resurrection on the vault of the apse is by Antoine Coypel.

Palaces of Germany and Austria

Germany

Schloss Benrath

Glimpsed from the woods or from the streets which approach it, Schloss Benrath, on the outskirts of Düsseldorf, looks like a gay summer pavilion, a child's birthday cake with pink icing. First appearances are misleading, for it is in every way a more substantial building, a genuine palace containing nearly 100 rooms, some of them of considerable size. It was built in the mid-18th century for the Elector Palatine, Karl Theodore, who later became elector of Bavaria. Thanks to this promotion and to the slow construction of the building (interrupted by the Seven Years' War), he occupied his delightful palace for only a short time. Later it became the headquarters of Napoleon's marshal, Murat, when he was grand duke of the short-lived duchy of Berg, and in the 19th century it was occasionally used as a summer palace by the Prussian royal family. Today it belongs to the city of Düsseldorf, whose officials had great difficulty in finding craftsmen of sufficient ability to restore the superb parquet floors, which must not be walked on except in soft slippers (provided at the door for visitors).

The main building is flanked by two crescent-shaped wings, standing slightly apart, with beautiful gardens dotted with statues, and a large ornamental pond. Concerts are sometimes given on the terrace.

The architect of this immensely enjoyable residence was a Frenchman, Nicolas de Pigage, who is not known for any comparable work elsewhere. The glorious Rococo plasterwork inside was most executed by German craftsmen. The swags and emblems, fauns and putti (enough of them, as one visitor remarked, to fill a fair-sized nursery school) might seem overwhelming were it not for the fact that the stucco is left ungilded and unpainted, while the overall riotous effect of the Rococo in full flight is here moderated by Classical influence.

The almost cottage-like proportions of Schloss Benrath, seen from certain points, are misleading. The interior displays Rococo decoration of exotic richness.

Schloss Benrath, said Monk Gibbon, is 'an architectural miracle; the perfect house for a large family of children; a residence considerably more solicitous for the comfort of its inhabitants than many of its epoch'.

Many of the rooms are oval or octagonal, and the task of drawing up the floor plan must have been challenging in the extreme. Some effort was saved by dividing the internal plan into two identical halves – rooms to the left of the main entrance precisely duplicating the rooms to the right. Here and there, as in the over-ingenious dome, sheer frivolity is in danger of taking over, and certainly Schloss Benrath is not a solemn building. Yet its sheer joyfulness is what makes it such a blessing in the rather serious environment of Düsseldorf.

Charlottenburg

The historic buildings of Berlin have suffered worse than most in modern times, and not only as a result of war. Today, Schloss Charlottenburg has been largely restored and in some respects enhanced – for instance, by Andreas Schlüter's splendid equestrian statue of the Great Elector, rescued from East Berlin where it was in danger of being melted down, and placed in the spacious courtyard.

Despite its fame and its considerable size, Schloss Charlottenburg is not, as royal palaces go, a

particularly striking building. It began as a rural mansion, 8 kilometres down the Charlottenburger Chaussee from the Brandenburg Gate, on the edge of the Spandauer Forest. It was built by the Elector Friedrich III for his wife, Sophie Charlotte, in the 1690s, and bore the name Lietzenburg. The Elector, by that time King Friedrich I, renamed the place when his wife died in 1705. The original building was then being enlarged, adopting an E-shaped plan around the courtyard. The architect responsible was a Swede, Johann Friedrich Eosander, who is said to have consulted the great Fischer von Erlach before drawing up his plans. The most striking feature of his work is the dome, raised on a very lofty octagonal drum and surmounted by a lantern with a wind vane in the form of a gilded statue of the goddess Fortuna. There is no doubt that those who complain that this structure is disproportionately high, especially when seen from the less monumental garden front, have a valid point; but few, surely, would wish it shorter.

The palace achieved the peak of its glory in the reign of Frederick the Great, who was responsible for the addition of perhaps its most famous feature, the Goldene Gallerie, destroyed in an air raid in 1943 less than 24 hours after it had been carefully photographed as insurance against that very calamity. It is from Frederick's time that the reputation of the Schloss as a great repository of art really dates, and a surprisingly large proportion of its fine collection of paintings, notably works by the masters of the French Rococo, Watteau and Boucher, are still to be seen there. Later additions include a number of adornments to the surrounding park and gardens, including the Classical mausoleum by Karl Friedrich Schinkel.

Above: In contrast with the rich Rococo decoration of Knobelsdorff's wing, built for Frederick the Great, this oval chamber at Charlottenburg emphasizes the virtues of restraint.

Left: Floodlighting at night emphasizes the unusual proportions of Schloss Charlottenburg, which is fronted by an immense courtyard containing Schlüter's equestrian statue of the Great Elector.

Herrenchiemsee

Many will know the bizarre story of Ludwig II of Bavaria. Deprived of real political power, he was determined to hold on to the role of the monarch as arbiter of culture and builder of palaces. His passion for Wagner helped to bring about the festival of Wagner's operas at Bayreuth, and for himself he sought to transform the most romantic elements of Wagner's works into facts of life, surrounding himself with representations of romantic myths based, none too closely, on Germany's medieval past. Few will not have seen, on German travel posters if nowhere else, pictures of Ludwig's romantic castles and grottoes at Linderhof, Neuschwanstein, and Herrenchiemsee.

Herrenchiemsee sprang not from Ludwig's weird involvement with German myth, however, but from his admiration for Louis XIV, the absolute monarch Ludwig himself would have liked to have been, and Herrenchiemsee was intended to be a more or less faithful copy of Versailles, to which, indeed, Ludwig made several visits incognito while his plans were being prepared. Building went ahead with amazing speed, from 1878, but the palace was not finished when, eight years later, the unfortunate Bavarian monarch was declared insane and his building projects halted.

Herrenchiemsee is a total phoney, magnificent but meaningless, a palace for an absolute monarch who did not exist on an island in a lake (the Chiemsee), remote and empty, quite uninhabited from Ludwig's time to the present. It is, nevertheless, magnificent, in some respects even more magnificent than Versailles itself. For instance, the Hall of Mirrors at Herrenchiemsee is nearly 100 metres (330 feet) long and lit by so many candles that an army of servants is needed to light them; if one person attempted the task, the first candle would have burned out by the time the last was lit. They are still lit, incidentally, for occasional concerts. Electricity has not intruded upon Herrenchiemsee.

The visitor needs a high degree of tolerance for aristocratic display and regal extravagance. There are, undeniably, many marvellous things. The porcelain chandelier in the dining room, the mould of which was destroyed on Ludwig's order so that no one should ever reproduce it, is certainly a magnificent work of art, and there is much that is enchanting in a fairy-tale kind of way. Nevertheless, in our more egalitarian age, it is difficult not to recoil before some of the excesses of Ludwig's extraordinary palace. In the royal bedroom, for example, it is impossible to imagine anyone ever getting a wink of sleep; even Ludwig only slept there for three weeks. Here is Baroque gone mad; a mass of gilded figures, scrolls, leafwork, emblems, velvet hangings and various conceits which almost totally obliterate the proportions of the room itself. In the dining room, the table sinks below the floor, so that the next course can be placed on it without a servant appearing in the room itself; latterly, Ludwig could not stand even the presence of servants

After the unification of Germany in 1870 the role of the Bavarian monarch was, to say the least, reduced. Ludwig II was determined to remain a great patron of art, and his unfinished palace at Herrenchiemsee emulated Versailles – the residence of a rather more powerful monarch than Ludwig.

The Hall of Mirrors at Herrenchiemsee —
perfect but pointless.

(admittedly, Louis XIV of France also had such a table). Though Ludwig dined alone on the 23 nights he spent at Herrenchiemsee, the table was set for four. The guests who did not appear were Louis XIV, Mme de Pompadour and Mme de Maintenon.

Ludwig preferred his fantastic Romanesque castle of Neuschwanstein. It was there, amid grand scenes from Wagnerian legend, that he spent his last years, alone and mad.

Imperial Palace, Goslar
Goslar, about 70 km south-east of Hanover and close to the present border between East and West Germany, is a charming medieval town romantically situated on the edge of the Harz Mountains. Its appearance of being almost untouched by time is a little misleading, since a great deal of restoration was done in the 19th century. Nevertheless, it was undamaged in World War II, and such gems as the old Rathaus (town hall), the Kaiserworth (formerly a guildhall) and the Kaiserhaus, or

imperial palace, remain to attract the visitor.

Political and economic circumstances combined to make Goslar a prosperous place in the Middle Ages. From the time of the Holy Roman Emperor, Henry III (1039–56), it was a favourite imperial residence; Henry's son (later the Emperor Henry IV) was born at Goslar, and the imperial diet (parliament) met there frequently. Goslar's second stroke of luck was the discovery of the rich metal ores of the Rammelsberg: silver, as well as lead, copper, zinc, and even a little gold have been mined since the 10th century, and an enormous silver pitcher in the Rathaus testifies to the ability of the silversmiths in the 15th century.

The Kaiserhaus is claimed to be the oldest secular building in Germany. Founded by Henry II and greatly enlarged by Henry III, it was partly burned down and rebuilt about 1289. Later alterations and enlargements did not enhance its appearance, but it was restored to something like its earlier state in 1878. Approached by a broad flight of steps, it consists basically of one block, the Saalbau, plus a wing connecting it to the chapel of St Ulrich, formerly the private chapel of the emperors and dating from the 11th century.

The imperial great hall (*Saal*) is on an upper floor, a tremendous room 50 metres (165 feet) long with seven large Romanesque windows overlooking the square (with its equestrian statues of Frederick Barbarossa and Wilhelm I). When the palace was restored, the walls were decorated with frescoes illustrating the development of the German Empire, a subject oddly contrasted with the story of the Sleeping Beauty, which appears above the windows. The ancient imperial throne, rescued from Goslar's famous cathedral (of which little remains), stands against one wall. A painted tomb in the Romanesque chapel contains the heart of Goslar's greatest patron, Henry III.

Schloss Langenburg, Württemburg

The makers of some cosy Hollywood movie about happy peasants in *lederhosen* could hardly design a more charming backdrop than that of Schloss Langenburg, which stands on a promontory looped by the River Jagst in Württemburg, West Germany. The courtyard especially is famous, not for the purity of its architecture but for a unique charm which is as much the result of happy accident as of careful plan. Though most of the palace dates from the Renaissance, the general impression is medieval, with projecting galleries, steep pitched roofs and octagonal tower; there are also apparently Baroque gables and Classical columns. Strange to say, there is not the least feeling of incongruity. The many fascinating and apparently disparate features come together to form a delightful and harmonious picture, with the tall clock tower forming the dominant point.

Schloss Langenburg originated in the 12th century as a chunky little fortress, and for a time it was the capital of the little principality of Hohenloe. The medieval fortress, with its four round towers built about the middle of the 13th century, still survives, having withstood several sieges with little apparent damage. In the late 16th and early 17th centuries, the fortress became a palace when a large though unpretentious mansion with a central courtyard appeared, linked to the medieval towers. Although there was considerable rebuilding in the 18th century, when the east end was expanded and a new entrance façade constructed, the building has changed very little since then.

The worst disaster suffered by Schloss Langenburg occurred less than a generation ago, in January 1963, when a fire destroyed the east end and one of the medieval towers. These have been completely rebuilt.

Below: Mounted German heroes of yesterday and tomorrow in the Kaiserpfalz (imperial district) of Goslar. The main building here is a modern reconstruction.

Bottom: The romantic courtyard of Schloss Langenburg. The tower has been heightened, but the builders left the original corbels in place, clearly indicating the original height.

Linderhof

Linderhof can be regarded as nothing more than a ridiculous anachronism, the self-indulgent fantasy of a monarch (Ludwig II of Bavaria) in less than total control of his mental faculties. When first built, in the 1870s, it aroused more scorn than admiration, but attitudes can change a good deal in one hundred years, and today Linderhof, despite some excesses like the grotto with its carefully modelled stalactites, the odd little Moorish building or the gilded nymphs frolicking in the pond, is usually seen as a work of art.

Its size – there are only four windows across the main façade – makes it a villa rather than a palace, but the flamboyant decoration is

A gilded fountain plays at Linderhof, perhaps the most successful of Ludwig's exercises in architectural nostalgia.

A touch of Moorish exoticism at Linderhof. The modest scale of the complex saves it from seeming too outlandish in its hilly, wooded setting.

truly palatial. It is in a sense a memorial to Ludwig's admiration for Louis XIV, expressed on a grander scale at Herrenchiemsee, and there are many reminders of the builder of Versailles. However, there is much more to it than imitation of French Baroque. It could have been built at no other time, and the French connection is largely misleading: the Rococo interiors owe as much to current South German style as to the France of Louis XIV or Louis XV.

This remarkable building derives much of its attraction from its splendid site, a spot which had nostalgic associations for Ludwig, in a wooded valley with mountains rising behind. A double flight of marble steps rises through the terraced gardens to a little Classical rotunda below the rockface, and the ancient lime tree from which the name Linderhof possibly derives was left in place by Ludwig's builders.

Nymphenburg

The 'castle of the nymphs', on the fringes of Munich, was the summer palace of the electors, later kings, of Bavaria. Like many other royal palaces, it is partly the result of the desire of lesser rulers to emulate Louis XIV's Versailles and, like Versailles, it is essentially an assembly of buildings in which some parts are more interesting than the whole.

The central block was the original unit, a compact, five-storeyed house resembling an Italian country villa and looking today much as it did when it was built by Agostino Barelli for Henrietta Adelaide of Savoy in the 1660s. Her son, the Elector Max Emanuel, added the blocks on either side, linked by narrow, colonnaded galleries. A Baroque park, with a canal leading to the centre of Munich, was laid out by a follower of André le Nôtre, and the interior of

Above: The royal bedchamber at Linderhof.
The Bavarian Rococo is too rich for some
tastes, but is executed with loving perfection.

Left: In contrast with the ethereal Rococo of
the rest of this captivating pavilion, the
kitchen of the Amalienburg is faced with
Dutch tiles in the *chinoiserie* fashion.

A view of the main front of the Nymphenburg palace from across the water. It is essentially an assembly of buildings on a modest scale linked by arcaded galleries.

the original house was altered to accommodate a great hall three storeys high. The arched windows in the façade were inserted at the same time. The addition of further buildings on the wings in the mid-18th century gave the assembly the general form of a crescent, enclosing a large courtyard.

The architect chiefly responsible for this layout was Josef Effner, a gardener's son sent to study in Paris by the Elector Max Emanuel. Effner also built two of the Rococo pavilions in the park which are perhaps more famous than the palace itself. The Pagodenburg was an early example of the fashion for 'Chinese' decoration: the exterior is of French

inspiration and the *chinoiserie* tiles on the ground floor came from Delft. The Badenburg (bath house) contains a tiled pool which is more swimming pool than bath. A third building, the Magdalenenklause, was built about the same time (the 1720s) as a kind of hermit's retreat, in the form of a grotto, grotesquely encrusted with stucco seaweed and coral.

The Amalienburg is, however, the most fascinating of the Nymphenburg's pavilions. Built as a hunting lodge (Diana is much in evidence) in the 1730s by François Cuvilliés, it has been described as 'the supreme secular monument of the Rococo'. In the glittering central

Mirror Room the mirrors, set at angles to one another, endlessly reflect the brilliant carved stucco and wood ornament. The Amalienburg is surely one of the most attractive pieces of decorative architecture in Europe.

Sans Souci

What an extraordinary man Frederick the Great was! The outstanding general of his time, who fought off most of Europe for six years and then, in an equivalent period, raised his country from war-torn ruin to become potentially the greatest state on the continent. An unlikely builder of delicate, fanciful palaces.

Potsdam is the heart of royal Prussia and its immediate associations are military. Frederick's Sans Souci is only one element in a large complex, not so large as the more conventional Neues Palais (also built by Frederick), and set amid a great variety of smaller contemporary and later structures; some of these, like the fantastic Chinese pavilion with its columns in the form of palm trees, are highly remarkable in themselves.

The general layout of Sans Souci, a summer residence set above a range of terraces, was roughed out by Frederick himself. The main entrance is fairly severely Classical,

The Amalienburg, the pavilion begun in 1734 by François Cuvilliés, has a basically simple though sophisticated exterior which makes a striking contrast with the ornamentation inside.

Right: A window in the library at Sans Souci, with glasshouses beyond. The woodwork is of warm, brown cedar, a rich background to the gilded Rococo ornament of Johann August Nahl.

Below: Sans Souci is a one-storey building apart from the low dome, its hilltop site bestowing splendid vistas nonetheless. The exterior hardly prepares the visitor for the exuberance of the interior.

the work of Georg von Knobelsdorf, and the brilliant Rococo decoration of the rooms beyond comes as a surprise. The little library, the music room and the Voltaire room (which the French philosopher probably never entered) display a fantasy of ornament, employing every conceivable material, which is unequalled anywhere else. Delicate, leafy, gilded forms (by Johann August Nahl and others) clamber over door panels, around windows and asymmetrical picture frames and mirrors, over walls and ceilings. Description makes it seem too elaborate; in fact, the German craftsmen never overstepped the bounds of good taste. The rooms may be stagey, but they are never vulgar.

Frederick's large bed-sitting room was redecorated in Neo-Classical style soon after his death in 1786. He had presumably approved the plans, and indeed his own tastes may have been changing. The armchair in which he died stands on the shimmering parquet floor, with his exquisite Louis XV writing desk nearby. The gardens, with fine statues including a typically French Venus, are as charming as the palace itself.

Ducal Palace, Weimar

The small city of Weimar, in the former state of Thuringia and now in East Germany, has a proud history. In this century it was the place where the well-meant though ill-fated republican constitution of 1919 was approved, and the original home of

the vastly influential Bauhaus school of design. Its greatest days were the late 18th and early 19th centuries, when it enjoyed a well-earned reputation as 'the German Athens'.

It was the Grand Duchess Anna Amalia who founded Weimar's reputation as the cultural capital of Germany, and the home of modern German literature, when she summoned the writer Christoph Wieland to the court in 1772. Under the Grand Duke Karl August, Goethe, Schiller, Herder and others soon followed.

The ducal palace, the most important building if not the most interesting in Weimar, was partially destroyed by fire in 1774. A remnant, including the tower, survives, but the main structure was rebuilt between 1789 and 1803 (it was not completely finished until much later owing to the interruption of the Napoleonic Wars – the battle of Jena took place within earshot). It has a fine Neo-Classical hall, but in general the palace, as an English visitor remarked, 'is imposing only from its extent'. Its construction was superintended by Goethe himself (possibly not so closely as tradition maintains), and he also designed the beautiful park on the banks of the River Ilm. Indeed, it is the literary associations of the palace which are most memorable. In one wing, the Herder Room is decorated with symbolic representations of that scholar's manifold intellectual interests; the Goethe Room and the Schiller Room have scenes from their works (rather

The old clock tower, the main survival from before the 18th-century reconstruction at Weimar, now welcomes the support of the later buildings abutting it.

an odd Mary Queen of Scots in the latter). Some minor artists of the Italian Renaissance are represented in the gracious apartments of the grand duke and duchess.

Residenz, Würzburg

The Residenz of the Prince-Bishop of Würzburg has been called 'the most important secular building in the Baroque style in Germany'. In view of the competition, this is praise of a high order. It was begun in 1720 for the newly appointed bishop, a member of the rich and powerful Schönborn family, and was structurally complete by 1744.

The splendour of the Residenz is the work of many people, not least the Prince-Bishops themselves, but the outstanding names associated with the building are those of Balthazar Neumann and Giovanni Battista Tiepolo. In 1720 Neumann was comparatively inexperienced, having recently returned from operations with the Austrian army, to which he was attached as a military engineer. His supreme building (apart from the Residenz), the church of Vierzehnheiligen, lay far in the future. It was therefore only natural that the Prince-Bishop should consult other experts besides

his protégé. They included neighbouring court architects such as Hildebrant (builder of the Belvedere in Vienna), and the Frenchmen De Cotte and Boffrand. Neumann, an architect of great ingenuity and catholic sympathies, benefited from their advice, and his building represents a fusion of Bohemian and Austrian Baroque with a dash of French Rococo. The most magnificent feature of the Residenz, the ceremonial staircase, is probably Neumann's conception entirely.

The decoration of the interior was most carefully considered. Eventually the Prince-Bishop (the fifth since the founder) decided to go to the top, and approached the Venetian painter Tiepolo, who was at the height of his fame. For a considerable fee, Tiepolo agreed to come, accompanied by his two sons, and in 1750–53 he completed the decoration of both the Great Hall and the vault of the staircase, where the theme chosen was the Four Continents. His brilliant exploitation of light, his marvellous colours – which seem to have fizzed out of some magic syphon – and his fertile imagination were never more splendidly displayed.

Left: Balthasar Neuman's magnificent Kaisersaal (Great Hall) at Würzburg was painted by Tiepolo with historical scenes, and is a splendid example of the way Baroque artists fused frescoes, stucco and architecture into a single unity.

Below: The central pavilion of the east façade of the Würzburg palace, seen from the terraces, where some of the sculpture amusingly parodies figures from Tiepolo's painting over the staircase.

Austria

Belvedere, Vienna

English or Dutch tourists who visit the 'garden palace' of Vienna come away with, among other impressions, a rather different idea of the War of the Spanish Succession from what they learned at school. For this was the residence of Prince Eugene of Savoy (1663–1736), the Austrian general whom English textbooks tend to describe as the very competent assistant of the Duke of Marlborough at Blenheim and other famous engagements. The guides at the Belvedere tell a different story. In Austria, the Prince is remembered as a tremendous hero who saved Europe from the Turks, defeated Louis XIV's hitherto invincible armies, and restored Habsburg power in central Europe. (The guides have heard of an English milord associated with Prince Eugene, but they are hazy about his name and rank.)

There are in fact two palaces, both splendid examples of Austrian Baroque architecture, of which the Lower Belvedere was the actual residence of the Prince while the far larger and more splendid Upper Belvedere was intended as nothing more than a staggering showpiece – to be admired but not lived in. The architect was Johann von Hildebrandt, who had served in the army under Eugene and has some claim to be considered at least the equal of those more famous exponents of Austrian Baroque, Fischer von Erlach and Jacob Prandtauer. Hildebrandt, however, had learned his trade largely in Italy, and what he created in the Belvedere was, in the characteristically apt words of Gordon Brook-Shepherd, 'a rare blend of Teutonic solidity and Mediterranean caprice'.

The interior of the larger building is even more impressive than the massive exterior – a dazzling Baroque assemblage in marble, gold and inlaid wood, created by a team of Italian artists hired by Hildebrandt.

Prince Eugene left no direct heir, and the Belvedere soon passed into the possession of the Habsburgs, who had even less use for it than he had. It acquired in time a rather gloomy reputation: it was the scene of Marie Antoinette's departure to become the queen of Louis XVI and thus fodder for the guillotine, and having remained empty for over a century, it became the home of the Archduke Franz Ferdinand, who left it in 1914 on a journey which ended abruptly in Sarajevo.

Schönbrunn Palace

The Schönbrunn, on the outskirts of Vienna, was the summer palace of

The imposing Baroque bulk of the Upper Belvedere palace, seen from the gardens below. It is the most striking example of a distinctively Austrian style which owed much to Italian traditions.

the Habsburgs during roughly the last third of their 600-year reign in Austria. A hunting lodge previously stood on the site, where the Emperor Maximilian had his menagerie in the early 16th century (there is still a zoo), but it was destroyed during the siege of Vienna by the Turks in 1683. As the threat of the Turks receded, the Emperor Leopold decided to build a grand palace there. The choice of architect can have caused little hesitation, for Fischer von Erlach (1656–1723) was already approaching the height of his reputation.

Nevertheless, his original plans were rejected: the Emperor wanted something grand but not *that* grand. A less expensive scheme was approved and the palace was more or less completed before the architect's death. Some alterations took place in the following generation under Nicolaus Pacassi, the effect of which was to reduce grandeur still further, since Fischer's trio of domes over the main entrance were removed. This has contributed to the comparatively unaggressive appearance of the palace, which though very large is less formidably imposing than any

other Baroque palace of comparable size.

There are other reasons for this pleasing impression: Fischer's staggered frontage, which brings the building forward at the wings as though inviting an approach; the golden-yellow colour of the palace, and, perhaps, the memory that the Schönbrunn's most famous resident was that most accommodating of empresses, Marie Theresa. She occupied it during the summer months nearly every year of her reign (1740–80), and the magnificent rooms echoed with the clatter of her enormous family.

It is not, however, easy to imagine cosy domesticity in the Schönbrunn, the main rooms of which are decorated in the highly elaborate Austrian Baroque style. The most striking interiors are those of the Great Gallery, with its tremendous symbolic frescoes on the ceiling, vast glittering chandeliers and inlaid floor; the adjoining Hall of Ceremonies, and the sparkling Hall of Mirrors. But many people find the smaller rooms, like the Yellow Drawing Room, no less attractive, and in their way hardly less splendid.

Marble staircase in the Upper Belvedere palace, with putti playing with the lamps, and atlantes (owing something to the tradition of Michelangelo) supporting the vault. The use of white marble has a lightening effect in this distinguished building.

Overleaf: Despite its size, the Schönbrunn is not a particularly formidable building, partly due to its genial colour. However, the removal of Fischer von Erlach's domes has not improved the original proportions.

Palaces of Italy and Greece

Italy

Barberini Palace, Rome

The Barberini family did not have a good reputation in Rome. They were the subject of a punning epigram comparing their rapacity with that of the *barbari* (barbarians), and they showed no compunction in plundering ancient buildings for items to ornament their own luxurious dwellings. Of Florentine origin, they acquired great wealth during the Renaissance and reached their height when Maffeo Barberini became pope as Urban VIII in 1623. The Palazzo Barberini, opposite the Quirinal Gardens on the Via delle Quattro Fontane, was begun two years later. It is, in terms of ostentatious splendour, probably the outstanding Baroque palace in Rome.

Three architects are chiefly associated with the building, Maderna, Bernini and Borromini, which is almost like a baptism conducted by the Holy Trinity. Maderna in fact died in the same year the work started, to be succeeded by Bernini; Borromini, who was related to Maderna, assisted them both. Architectural historians have debated lengthily the question of who was responsible for what in the Barberini palace, and the commonest opinion is that Maderna's plans were carried out by his successors without fundamental deviation. The most

The Palazzo Barberini is certainly one of the grandest palaces in Rome, which is hardly surprising in view of the eminent architects associated with it. Today it is an art gallery.

notable feature, however, the great central portico with two rows of seven large arched windows above, is probably the work of Bernini, as is the more orthodox, rectangular staircase; the subtle oval staircase on the other side of the building appears to be one of Borromini's contributions.

The general plan is more characteristic of rural villas than Roman palaces, taking the form of an H, with no courtyard. The great hall has a famous allegorical ceiling fresco, the masterpiece of Pietro da Cortona, an exponent of the most extravagant illusionist Baroque decoration in early 17th-century Italy.

Today the state apartments are occupied by the collections of the National Gallery of Rome. The more popular name is the Barberini Gallery, which is only just since, besides the actual premises, many of the paintings once belonged to the Barberini family.

Caserta

The palace of Caserta, north of Naples, is perhaps the most ambitious of all efforts to rival Versailles. A rectangular block, 250 × 190 metres (820 × 625 feet) with four internal courtyards, it was built, like Versailles, for a Bourbon dynasty. Charles III, who commissioned it, was a great-grandson of Louis XIV. In appearance it is not particularly reminiscent of Versailles except in size, and being constructed at a time when the Baroque was giving way to Neo-Classicism, it is somewhat severe. The original architect,

Luigi Vanvittelli, was of Dutch descent; he had studied under Filippo Juvarra and built up a considerable reputation in Rome. Caserta, though grand enough, was even grander in Vanvittelli's original but too expensive scheme, which included square towers at the corners and a central dome on the high drum.

The building was to be linked with Naples by a great avenue 30 km long. The park behind was designed to be even larger than it is now, with a watercourse, supplied by an aqueduct 40 km long, continuing the line of the avenue. Mythological sculptural groups, notably of Diana and Actaeon, are set in the landscape like stage tableaux, with an assortment of lavish fountains.

Except for a few Rococo rooms, like the Queen's Bathroom, the decoration, though rich, is comparatively austere. The state apartments, which are now open to the public, date mostly from a later period. The magnificent Throne Room was completed in a hurry in 1845 to impress the delegates to an international scientific conference. Other apartments reflect the influence on Neo-Classicism of the discoveries at Pompeii and Herculaneum.

Farnese Palace, Rome

The illustrious Farnese family figured in Italian politics as early as the 11th century, but achieved the height of their wealth and power in 16th-century Rome. The beauty of Giulia Farnese ensnared the pope, Alexander VI, who heaped honours and riches on her family. He made

When all is said and done, perhaps the most impressive feature of the royal palace of Caserta is its sheer size. It has been said that one may walk in it all day without passing the same spot twice.

her brother Alessandro a cardinal and in 1534 Alessandro himself became pope as Paul III. One of his grandsons, Alessandro (a cardinal at 14), was chiefly responsible for completing the Farnese palace.

The Palazzo Farnese, a great rectangular block around a central courtyard, is the grandest Renaissance palace in Rome. Begun in 1534, it is the masterpiece of Antonio Sangallo, member of a Florentine family of artists and one of the leading architects of the Roman Renaissance. When he died in 1546 his work was taken over by Michelangelo (who also succeeded him as chief architect of St Peter's), and the finishing touches were supplied by Giacomo della Porta.

The façade of the palace presents a subtle illustration of the contrasting styles of Sangallo and Michelangelo. The lower two storeys, sober, static and Classically Roman, are by Sangallo. The upper storey was added by Michelangelo who, while superficially following the same tradition, added a touch of dynamic fluidity, a definite suggestion of the Baroque.

The grave magnificence of Sangallo is again apparent as you enter the palace through a splendid barrel-vaulted vestibule, flanked by columns. Walking straight through, you emerge in the harmonious *cortile* (courtyard), with its restful arcades. A ceremonial staircase leads to the main apartments and the enormous, two-storeyed room where the Farnese collection of antique sculpture was formerly displayed. The single most famous decorative feature – a significant work in the history of European art – is the ceiling painted by the great Bolognese artist Annibale Carracci (1560–

The famous ceiling painting of Annibale Carracci in the Palazzo Farnese, which was a model for the decorators of French palaces in the 17th century.

Right: The complex system of perspectives in the royal palace of Caserta, in which a cool, even severe Neo-Classical style is dominant.

1609) with scenes of the love affairs of the gods derived from Ovid.

Since the great days of the Farnese, their palace has been inhabited by a variety of famous and not-so-famous people, including that brilliant but wayward monarch, Christina of Sweden, who gave up her throne in 1654 in order to practise her religion and indulge her intellectual interests in Rome. For the past hundred years or so the palace has served as the French embassy.

Doria Palace, Genoa

The west side of the Piazza del Principe, close to the old harbour of Genoa, is occupied by the lengthy façade of the Doria Palace. It is a memorial to the most famous member of a great Genoese family, Andrea Doria (?1468–1560), a great admiral and commander of the fleet of Charles V, to whom it was presented in 1522 by his admiring fellow-citizens.

It is sometimes forgotten that in the Middle Ages Genoa was a Mediterranean sea power of equivalent rank to Venice. In 1380 the Genoese inflicted a terrible defeat on the Venetians, but their independence, always precarious, appeared to be lost for good under French domination until, in the 1520s, Andrea Doria restored the republic and gave it a government which lasted without fundamental change for nearly three centuries.

According to an inscription on the wall of the palace, Andrea Doria decided to rebuild it, for himself and his successors, as a way of closing his career in honourable repose. This reconstruction took place about 1530, to designs by Fra Giovanni Angelo Montorsoli.

The great admiral himself appears in the guise of Poseidon in a sculptured fountain in the gardens that flank the spacious courtyard. There are numerous family portraits and some fine frescoes (restored in the

The French Embassy in Rome, better known as the Palazzo Farnese, which was originally built for the future Counter-Reformation Pope, Alessandro Farnese (Paul III).

73

Right: A monument to the pride of Genoa, the Palazzo Doria contains sumptuous interior ornament of several periods.

Below: A view of the Doria Palace from the gardens; the figure of Poseidon bears the features of the great admiral himself.

19th century) by Penno del Vaga (1501–47), a painter of the Florentine school who had assisted Raphael in Rome. The stucco and painted decoration of the main gallery shows an unmistakable relationship with Raphael's loggias in the Vatican.

Ducal Palace, Mantua

Mantua during the Renaissance was one of the liveliest artistic and intellectual centres in northern Italy. It owed its position to the efforts of a remarkable dynasty, the Gonzaga. Though less well-known than the Medici of Florence or the Sforza of Milan, they are in some ways the most fascinating of all the great Renaissance dynasties, rising from peasant stock to achieve power and (eventually) a ducal title in what was then the island-city of Mantua. They were patrons and collectors on a lavish scale, and the ducal palace, one of several Gonzaga palaces, is probably the biggest and grandest building of its kind in Italy.

The palace still retains its early 14th-century Gothic façade, but it was frequently altered and enlarged by the Gonzaga, especially during the time of Federico II (1519–40). His architect was Giulio Romano, who also built the Palazzo del Te as a honeymoon home and summer villa, decorating the walls with erotic frescoes. Giulio Romano's bold, Mannerist style accounts for the paired, twisted columns and for the archways giving a view of the lake in the Cortile della Cavallerizza.

Although many of the treasures of the Gonzaga have been long dispersed, there is still much to admire, including frescoes by Giulio Romano and his pupils, woodwork and stucco ornament by Primaticcio, busts by Bernini, some fine Venetian glass, a chamber of the Zodiac with a slightly obscene ceiling painting of the Signs by Lorenzo Costa, and the charming early Renaissance work in the chambers of Isabella d'Este, the greatest female patron of the Renaissance in Italy.

The palace contains about 500 rooms and has stabling for 600 horses; some staircases were designed for horses to spare their riders the fatigue of climbing them on foot.

An 18th-century room in the Ducal Palace, Mantua, the Chamber of the Rivers.

Among other remarkable features are an enormous roof garden, a highly informative astrological clock which recommends times for mending clothes or going on a journey, and apartments built to scale for the dwarfs of whom the Gonzaga were so fond (possibly because many of the Gonzaga themselves were hunchbacks).

Medici-Riccardi Palace, Florence

On Florence's Via Cavour, hectic with traffic, stands the building which is most closely associated with the wonderfully prolific flowering of genius in the Florentine Renaissance. Though usually known nowadays after its later owners as the Palazzo Riccardi, this overpoweringly massive building was the home of the Medici during the 15th and 16th centuries.

Lorenzo the Magnificent was born and kept his brilliant court here, where Michelangelo first tried out his sculptor's chisel and the members of the Platonic academy were royally entertained. The building was erected between about 1444 and 1460 for Cosimo the Elder, and it is the best-known work of the sculptor and architect Michelozzo di Bartolommeo (1396–1472).

Michelozzo is renowned for the lightness and elegance of his style, evident, for example, in the Medici villa at Fiesole, but the exterior of the Palazzo Riccardi shows little sign of those qualities. The frontage is distinctly forbidding. In this, the earliest true Renaissance palace in Florence, Michelozzo first adopted the system of graduated rustication, in which the lowest storey is very heavily rusticated so that, from an angle, it looks almost as if it had been assembled without mortar from undressed stones, while the middle storey is constructed of lightly channelled stone and the uppermost storey is almost completely smooth. The building is crowned by an elaborate cornice, incorporating an attractive arrangement of Classical motifs.

In 1659 the palace was sold to the Riccardi, and it was later altered and extended at one end: there are now

Top: Since it is in Mantua, rather than Florence, Rome or another of the cities favoured by tourists, the palace of the Gonzaga receives less attention than it deserves, for it is arguably the most impressive of all the great palazzi of the Italian ducal families.

Above: From the cathedral, situated on high ground, there is a splendid view of Mantua's Ducal Palace.

Right: One of Gozzoli's famous frescoes of the Journey of the Wise Men in the Medici-Riccardi Palace. A number of Medici portraits are included and the artist himself appears among the followers.

Left: The Palazzo Medici-Riccardi was both a family residence and the headquarters of the Medici commercial operations. Some of the arches at the corners were originally open.

17 windows on the second storey whereas the original building had only ten. But its essential character remained unchanged. It passed into the hands of the state in the early 19th century.

Michelozzo's interior plan was more characteristically elegant, with the rooms arranged around an open, arcaded *cortile* and the main apartments on the *piano nobile* or principal floor (the second storey), reached by a fine staircase. The most notable works of art in the palace are, without doubt, the famous frescoes painted by Benozzo Gozzoli in 1463 in the little Medici Chapel, illustrating the Journey of the Magi.

The Pitti Palace was the residence of the Medici grand dukes of Tuscany and their successors of the House of Lorraine for about three centuries. Ammanati's heavily rusticated garden façade was imitated in several other buildings.

Pitti Palace, Florence

The early Renaissance palaces of Florence are not, on the whole, buildings of obvious beauty. The mightily rusticated stonework and rather mean windows of the Pitti or the Strozzi make them look less like a wealthy family's mansion than a municipal prison, but of course their purpose was not to confine the inhabitants within but to keep their enemies out. Though not built, like the castles of the Middle Ages, to withstand a siege, they were intended to be impregnable to stone-throwing mobs or the armed bands of rival clans. Hence their forbidding, fortress-like appearance.

The Pitti Palace is now a museum – or rather several museums. The Galleria Palatina, its rooms named after the planets, contains about 500 Renaissance and Baroque paintings, with many works by Raphael, Titian and others of like stature.

The Palazzo Pitti, on rising ground near the Ponte Vecchio, was begun for Luca Pitti in 1458. The original plans were allegedly by Filippo Brunelleschi, the first great Renaissance architect, best known for the dome of Florence cathedral, but he was already dead when the palace was begun. Only the central block, up to the second storey, was built by 1466, when the decline of the Pitti put an end to construction. Eleanor of Toledo, wife of the Medici Duke Cosimo I, had the palace enlarged and completed in the mid-16th century by Bartolommeo Ammanati, who built the somewhat grotesquely rusticated garden façade, overlooking the famous Boboli gardens. Further extensions were added in the 17th century, and the projecting outer wings were built, at some cost to the symmetry of the building, in the 18th century. These additions made the Pitti probably the largest – certainly the most imposing – palace in Italy outside the Vatican.

The Pitti's fame as an art gallery dates from the late 18th century, when the public was first admitted. The collection is second only in Florence to the Uffizi, and is, naturally, especially rich in paintings of the Florentine Renaissance, though it also contains a dozen Raphaels, a large number of the best Venetians and some splendid Rubens. The Pitti, which is really five separate museums, also contains the treasures collected by the Medici grand dukes, a gallery of modern Tuscan art, and a coach museum.

Royal Palace, Naples

Until the unification of Italy in the 19th century, the city of Naples was capital of a kingdom, which in the 16th century was part of the Spanish dominions. The royal palace was commissioned by the Spanish viceroy and designed by Domenico Fontana, who before his official appointment as 'royal engineer' in Naples had acquired some fame in Rome as the architect of, among other buildings, the Quirinal palace. Work began in 1600 and, although the palace was not completed until the early 18th century, it followed Fontana's original plan. A large part of it had to be rebuilt in the early 19th century after a serious fire, and at that time the palace was enlarged. The imposing statues of the rulers of Naples from Norman times onwards, which adorn the lower storey of the main façade, were placed there in the 1880s.

It is an enormous building. The frontage of the 18th-century wing on the Bay of Naples stretches over 200 metres (655 feet) and rises 30 metres (98 feet) in three receding stages from the rusticated lower storey. The entrance façade, the oldest part, is less overwhelming in scale and more elegant in detail. It is, however, the colour which is the most immediately striking feature of the building. It is painted a strong shade of red, with green shutters.

Despite this superficial brilliance, the royal palace is somehow a sombre building, and this impression is reinforced by the interior, which is luxurious but gloomy. There is little furniture. The state rooms are impressive, especially the throne room with its broad coving of gilded stucco figures and marble floor in hexagonal pattern which dates from about 1840. There are a large number of paintings, notably by followers of Caravaggio, frescoes celebrating the victories of Spanish arms and panels of incidents from *Don Quixote*.

Quirinal, Rome

The former summer home of the popes is approximately fifteen minutes' walk from the Vatican; however, as it is set on the Quirinal hill, it is often cooler, and it commands a splendid view of Rome. The palace, which is very large and rather complex, was begun by Gregory XIII in 1583 and continued under his immediate successors. The finest Roman artists of the Mannerist or early Baroque period were employed in its construction and decoration, and it also includes antique and Renaissance works, such as the Classical figures of *The Horse-tamers*, found originally in the Baths of Constantine.

The original buildings are mainly the work of Carlo Maderna and Domenico Fontana, who built the main front and the façade over-looking the piazza (except for the entrance portal, designed by Flaminio Ponzio with later embellishment by Bernini). Ponzio also designed the Pope's private chapel (Capella dell'Annunciata), which contains

Below: The Audience Chamber of the Royal Palace in Naples. The effect is severe: the marble floors are chilling and the chandeliers downright threatening.

Bottom: This wing of the Royal Palace at Naples, on the landward side, masks the immense size of the building which dominates the Bay of Naples.

Above: The main approach to the Castello di Stupinigi, one of the most exciting buildings of the Late Baroque, built by Juvarra as a hunting lodge for the kings of Savoy.

Above left: The summer palace of the popes on the Quirinal, the highest of the Seven Hills of Rome, has a lengthy wing, the *manica lunga* ('long sleeve') along the Via del Quirinale.

Left: Detail of the sensational Great Hall at Stupinigi, with frescoes by Domenico and Giuseppe Valeriani.

beautiful paintings by Guido Reni and others members of the Bolognese school. The highly elaborate Sala Regia (or Sala de Corazzieri) designed, together with the adjoining public chapel, by Maderna, is without doubt the most arresting chamber; it contains ornamental contributions by Bernini and Agostino Tassi, and its marble floor reflects the gilded stucco ceiling and Tassi's painted frieze, in which human figures appear to be leaning out of windows overlooking the room. Among other rooms of special interest are the 18th-century Mirror room in the Chinese style and a beautiful little library of the same period, with inlaid ivory and mother-of-pearl in a delicate Rococo arrangement.

The gardens, little changed since the early 17th century, have statues, fountains, palms, orange trees and lawns, enclosed by box hedges of military cut, as well as a little Palladian coffee house and an organ played by water.

The Quirinal palace was used by popes hoping to escape the heat and malaria of the Vatican until the late 19th century, when it was appropriated by the king of Italy. Today it is occupied by the president of the republic.

Stupinigi

The hunting lodge of the kings of Sardinia known as Stupinigi, near Turin, is the secular masterpiece of the great Piedmontese architect, Filippo Juvarra (1678–1736). A hunting lodge, in 18th-century Europe, could mean almost anything and Stupinigi is a grand, magnificent building, perhaps the finest example of the North Italian Late Baroque in secular architecture.

The buildings are grouped around a large hexagonal courtyard. The main block is star-shaped in plan and consists of a great central, domed oval, with powerfully projecting wings at an angle to the main axis. On the very top is a large statue of a stag, and beyond the formal gardens and terraces the deer park stretches into the distance.

Inside, the principal feature is the Great Hall, where four large fluted piers support a curving balcony and, above, the dome is painted with a scene of Diana, goddess of the chase, preparing to go hunting. Here, Juvarra's cool, classicizing form of Baroque is perfectly blended with his gift for theatrical effect.

Magnificent though it is, Stupinigi actually represents a slightly more modest version of Juvarra's original plan, but by the time it was finished, the architect and his original patron were both long dead. Many of the apartments date from the late 18th century, when some very lavish parties were given in the palace – the Great Hall then serving as a ball-room. After the Napoleonic up-heavals (the Emperor himself slept in one of the more austere bedrooms and for a time his sister, Pauline Borghese, lived there), it returned to the kings of Savoy, who used it periodically throughout the 19th century. Badly damaged during World War II, it has since been fully restored.

Royal Palace, Turin

The royal palace of Turin, residence of the kings of Sardinia, stands in the centre of the city. Though immense, its general exterior appearance is plain and uninspiring; but this impression is misleading, as it contains rooms which for sheer luxury of adornment have few equals any-where in Europe. It was begun about the middle of the 17th century and the main block was completed by 1663, but work continued through-out much of the 18th and 19th centuries.

In 1666 Giovanni Guarini (1624–83), one of the most imaginative architects of any age, was summoned to the palace to complete the half-built chapel of SS Sindone, the resting place of that holiest of relics, the Turin Shroud (in which Jesus is be-lieved to have been buried). Guarini crowned the chapel with its famous dome, a geometric gem of a structure which has fascinated architects ever since.

Guarini marks the beginning of a brilliant period in Piedmontese architecture in the late 17th and early 18th centuries. After him came Filippo Juvarra (1678–1736), who entered royal service in 1714 and remained in Turin until his death. Among Juvarra's works in the royal palace are the Chinese Room, with its delicately carved scrollwork in red and gold, and the so-called Scissor Staircase. He was also responsible for hiring artists and craftsmen of great skill, like Pietro Piffeti, who carried the art of marquetry to new lengths, choosing rare woods inlaid with ivory and precious metals. The Mirror Room, all gilt and glass, with little framed portraits painted directly on the glass, dates from shortly after Juvarra's time. Some of the most imposingly ornate, though not the most attractive, rooms, including the Throne Room and the Council Chamber, were created in the 19th century under the direction of a Bolognese artist, Pelagio Pelagi.

Urbino

The features of Duke Federigo da Montefeltro – that tremendously hooked nose and square, intelligent head – are familiar to every student of the early Renaissance, and his court at Urbino, if not quite as glam-orous as that of the Medicis in Flor-ence or the d'Estes in Ferrara, was one of the liveliest centres of Renais-sance culture.

The ducal palace, which is Federigo's greatest memorial, commands a hilltop site in one of the most attractive of Italian medieval towns. Widely regarded at the time as the ideal princely residence, the palace is almost a city within a city, a massive but beautiful building, somewhat irregular in appearance

The extraordinary dome of Guarini's Capella della SS Sindone peeps a little incongruously above the severe Classical façade of the Royal Palace in Turin.

due partly to the nature of the site and partly to the architect's use of contrasting features to add life and vigour. It was built by the Dalmatian, Luciano da Laurana, who, if not quite in the class of Bramante (a native of Urbino), was a man of great accomplishment, capable of princely displays of magnificence but also very sensitive to the most subtle effects of light. From a distance, the appearance is Gothic, with the turrets of the tall round towers that guard the entrance framed against the sky. Once in the beautiful courtyard, with its graceful Corinthian colonnade, the emphasis is Classical. It has been suggested that Piero della Francesca may have had some influence on the design: he was certainly resident in Urbino and may have written his famous work on perspective there.

Of the apartments, the largest is the Throne Room, where the architect ensured a pure but subdued light by arranging for all the windows to face north. Everywhere, the sculptured doorways and friezes are especially fine, but the most fascinating room, quite a small one, is the study of Duke Federigo himself, with its brilliant illusionist marquetry – some of it said to have been based on designs by Botticelli, and executed by Baccio Pontelli – and beautifully carved, pierced wooden panels, doors and ceiling, the latter painted in bright colours.

Doges' Palace, Venice

There is no other city like Venice, and no palace like the doges' palace which, adjoining the great church of

Above: Duke Federigo had the old fortress of Urbino reconstructed in 1465 by Luciano da Laurana, 'a man more skilled in architecture founded upon arithmetic and geometry than any in Tuscany, that fountain of architects...'

Left: The Duke's Study at Urbino. The exquisite marquetry was based on designs by Botticelli.

Overleaf: The Sala del Maggior Consiglio is the largest and most impressive of the state apartments in the Doges' Palace, Venice. At the far end is Tintoretto's enormous painting of *Paradise*.

St Mark, overlooks the lagoon. It is essentially Venetian Gothic, and that alone explains its uniqueness, since the Gothic style in Venice, a city that always looked east as well as west, is highly individual in character.

The first palace on this site was built in the 9th century, if not earlier, and recent discoveries suggest that it may have been almost as big as the present building, which was begun in 1340. The façade seen from the lagoon was finally completed early in the 15th century and the matching wing, facing west, was built a generation later.

Although her days of glory were numbered, Venice was still the capital of an immensely successful commercial empire in the 15th century, and the palace, which was the seat of government and the state prison as well as the doge's residence, proclaimed Venetian pride and prosperity. The main façades consist of three storeys, the lower two being open arcades; the upper storey (rebuilt in the late 16th century after a particularly damaging fire) is faced with pink and white marble forming a pattern of crosses set in diamonds. Inside the main entrance is the ceremonial Giants' Staircase, guarded by Jacopo Sansovino's splendid figures of Neptune and Mars, symbolizing Venetian dominance of sea and land.

The palace is equally renowned for the sumptuous character of the state apartments, of which the Sala del Maggior Consiglio is the largest and grandest. Tintoretto's vast painting of *Paradise*, which covers one entire wall, is claimed by the guides to be the largest painting of its type in the world. The overpoweringly elaborate early-Baroque ceiling was also decorated by Tintoretto. The ceiling of the marble-columned Sala delle Quattro Porte is even more ornate, though some of Tintoretto's paintings have been too enthusiastically restored.

Among other treasures, the palace contains works by most of the great artists of the Venetian school, though many were lost, along with the original furniture, in a fire in 1577. The prison now houses sculpture.

The west façade of the Doges' Palace follows the scheme of the 14th-century south façade, though built a century later. The patterned walls of the upper storeys suggest some fine silk fabric such as Venetian merchants dealt in.

Greece

Royal Palace, Corfu

The royal palace of Corfu, more correctly the Palace of St Michael and St George, has a curious though short history. When the Ionian Islands became a British protectorate in 1815, a suitable residence was required for the High Commissioner. Also needed was a meeting place for the legislative assembly and a headquarters for the recently founded British Order of St Michael and St George, originally restricted to those who had performed some special service in the Mediterranean area. The palace fulfilled all these roles.

Built in a creamy Maltese stone – now rather flaked and stained – it is a simple building which tactfully adopts the Classical Greek style. On the main façade, a shady Doric colonnade runs the length of the building, which is flanked by arches in the Roman triumphal manner (a

road now runs through one of them). Originally, there was a figure of Britannia above the central pediment.

The architect of the palace was George Whitmore, at the time a colonel in the Royal Engineers attached to the British garrison. The state rooms on the second storey consist of an elegant central, circular chamber with a dome decorated with Wedgwood 'jasperware' (white raised on a blue ground) plaques, with Classical statues on plinths of bluish marble; a dining room; and a throne room, containing a well-known portrait of George IV by Lawrence and slightly comical ones of St Michael and St George.

In the late 19th century, and more recently, the palace was used as a royal residence, in conjunction with the royal villa, Mon Repos, nearby. By the end of the Greek Civil War it was in a very dilapidated condition, but it has been sympathetically restored by a local architect and now serves as a museum.

The main façade of the Royal Palace in Corfu, with its fine Doric colonnade and the arch, just visible at the left, through which the road passes.

Palaces of Spain and Portugal

Spain

The Alhambra

The Alhambra, the outstanding achievement of the Nasrid dynasty in Muslim Spain, is one of the most famous buildings in the world. With the Cordoba mosque and the Taj Mahal, it is certainly one of the three most beautiful buildings of Islam, if not the world. It stands on a rocky hill overlooking the city of Granada, and from a distance it looks like an impregnable fortress, the austerity of its square towers and battlements totally concealing the extraordinary richness and delicacy within. It is a vastly complicated building, on a curiously irregular plan which does not seem to have been dictated merely by the site, and it is easy to get lost among the numerous courtyards, halls, arches and watercourses. The compulsion of Muslim architects to make buildings that appear to dissolve before the eyes, never realized more successfully than here, can have an almost dizzying effect. As you stand in the Chamber of the Two Sisters, looking up into the cupola, the intricate honeycomb vault with its myriads of *mukkarnas* (stalactites) appears not as something fashioned from solid material by the hands of men but as an optical illusion achieved by the manipulation of light.

This astonishing palace is really indescribable – for two reasons. Its size and complexity cannot be encompassed by a guided tour in print, however lengthy, and its decorative effect far surpasses a mundane description of the ornamental components. The main central elements are two courtyards, the Alberca or Court of Myrtles, and

From a distance, the Alhambra appears as an impregnable hilltop fortress (sharing the site with a later, Renaissance palace) and offers no hint of the delicate ornament within.

Above: Pools, palm trees and delicate arches — characteristic motifs of the serene palace of the Nasrids in Granada.

Left: A view of the famous Lion Court of the Alhambra, the centre of the area reserved for the harem. The use of alternate single and double columns in the arcades is a typical example of the sophisticated elegance achieved by the Muslim designers.

A detail of the Court of Myrtles in the Alhambra, which shows how the intricate delicacy of the abstract and calligraphic ornament dispels the solidity of stone.

the Lion Court, in the area reserved for the harem and giving entrance to the Chamber of the Two Sisters, probably the finest single chamber in the palace, with a private garden beyond. Flowers, trees and water played important parts in the overall effect. The famous Lion Court, with its central fountain supported by sculpted lions (a rare example of free-standing sculpture in Islamic art) was once a mass of foliage and blossom, augmenting the delicate abstract and calligraphic patterns of the walls. The only dissonant note in this marvellous assemblage is the roof of rounded tiles, which appears too heavy for the slender columns and arches below; the roof, it need hardly be said, is a recent addition.

The Salon de los Espejos, or Hall of Mirrors, in the royal palace of Aranjuez, near Madrid.

The Alhambra was built mainly in the 14th century, the labour provided, according to legend, by Christian slaves, but almost nothing is known of its builders. There is a clear debt to contemporary North African architecture, though the Alhambra, with its serene spaces and calm richness, surpasses any building in the Maghreb. The palace was in its day a citadel, centre of a vigorous kingdom, and it witnessed incidents that seem inappropriate in these peaceful surroundings – sons decapitated at their father's order, devious plots and, at the end, grim bitterness as the kingdom of Granada, the last Muslim outpost in Spain, fell to the Most Catholic monarchs in 1492.

Aranjuez

The royal palace of Aranjuez on the River Tagus, near the point where it is joined by the Jarama about 50 km south of Madrid, has a pleasantly unified appearance which, as is often the case with great palaces, belies its rather complicated architectural history. In the Middle Ages, there was a castle here belonging to the Knights of St James, an order prominent in the Spanish crusades against the Muslims. It passed into the possession of the Most Catholic

kings, Ferdinand and Isabella, in the late 15th century, and Charles V converted it into a hunting lodge. His son, Philip II, had a country palace built by the architects of the Escorial and grew very attached to it. Unfortunately, fire, that potent foe of historic architecture, destroyed the palace on at least two occasions. The present structure dates from the middle of the 18th century, when it was largely rebuilt by Santiago Bonavia, an architect of Italian origin, for that most melancholy of Spanish monarchs, Ferdinand VI.

It is a long, low building, only two storeys high except for the main block, and occupying three sides of a large courtyard. The wings, with terraced roofs and galleries, were built somewhat later, but faithfully followed the subdued Rococo style of Bonavia's main block. The latter is of three units, the arcaded pediment with statues of Spanish kings. At the two corners, shallow domes (said to have been influenced by Filippo Juvarra), topped by lanterns, and placed on drums pierced with circular windows, augment the general air of quiet distinction.

The interior is more of a jumble, and contains some odd features, like the pseudo-Moorish smoking room –

Right: It is easy to see why Philip II, who turned his father's hunting lodge of Aranjuez into a country palace, should have felt a special affection for it, coming from his more formidable residence in the Escorial.

The Hall of Battles in the Escorial is a gallery over 50 metres (150 feet) long painted with scenes of Spanish victories. The ceiling was decorated in the 18th century in the style inspired by recent discoveries at Pompeii.

founded the Royal Monastery of St Lawrence. He placed it in a starkly magnificent setting 1,000 metres (3,280 feet) above sea level on the slopes of the Sierra de Guadarrama, about 50 km from Madrid. The complex of buildings, which includes monastery, palace, school and mausoleum, is universally known by the name of the little village of el Escorial ('the slagheap') which housed the workmen and monks during construction. It was mainly completed between 1563 and 1584, a remarkably short time in view of its size, and although nearly every subsequent Spanish monarch, especially Ferdinand VII (1803–33), added something, they did not change the main features of the Escorial.

The general exterior is best seen from a distance, when the size and proportions of this granite fortress of Spanish Catholicism can best be appreciated. The combination of imposing grandeur and bleak austerity owes a great deal to the temper of Philip II himself, who supervised the plans at every stage and commanded his architects to observe 'simplicity in construction, severity in the total effect; nobility without arrogance, majesty without ostentation'. The achievement of the Escorial could not be better described.

The basic plan is a huge rectangle, approximately 200 × 160 metres (655 × 525 feet). The blankness of the unornamental façades is

the colours rather bright – added in the late 19th century for Alfonso XII, and, of far greater interest, the dazzling porcelain room, in which there is no escape from the vivid products of the Buen Retiro factory since the only spaces not covered by porcelain tiles are occupied by mirrors.

The Escorial

In gratitude for the victory over the French at the Battle of St Quentin on the Saint's feast day in 1557, Philip II

relieved – slightly – by the square towers at the corners and a Classical portico on the main, western front. In the east, a block of royal apartments around a courtyard projects to form, allegedly, the handle of the 'gridiron' – the instrument of St Lawrence's martyrdom which the outline plan is said to represent. The main building within the rectangle is the domed basilica church, which strongly resembles St Peter's, Rome. The church occupies a central position on the eastern side and its main entrance, adorned with gigantic statues of the kings of Judah, overlooks the Court of the Kings, which in turn adjoins the main portico. On either side of this central axis, the buildings are grouped around a series of courtyards – ten of them (the gridiron again) including the cloisters next to the church.

Needless to say, the Escorial contains great treasures, including paintings by the Dutch masters, of whom Philip II was unexpectedly fond, and by Titian, El Greco and Velasquez. The library is famous and, though depleted over the years, is probably still the greatest Renaissance library in Europe, with many Arabic manuscripts. Among other interesting features are the Hall of Battles, a gallery of feats of Spanish arms; the little room with a window through which the dying Philip II could observe the Mass; an 18th-century chamber decorated in the Pompeian fashion, and the royal tombs in the Pantheon of the Kings.

In 1671 fire raged through the Escorial for two weeks and, although the church and one or two other buildings escaped, the damage was enormous. Scarcely less devastating was its looting by French troops in 1808, while another fire, in 1872, destroyed part of the library and other treasures. Many once-reported

The ornate burial vault or Pantheon of the Kings at the Escorial. Philip II is second from the top on the left, below his father, the Emperor Charles V.

Left: The superbly vaulted library in the Escorial is a tribute to the learning of the Middle Ages: the ceiling frescoes are based on a medieval educational theme.

The Palace of Charles V in Granada, next door (so to speak) to the Alhambra, shows an assured comprehension of the principles of Classical Renaissance architecture as evolved in Italy.

items from the collections of Philip II and later monarchs, including a feather from the wing of the Archangel Gabriel, have disappeared at one time or another, their fate unrecorded; but the Escorial remains the most impressive monument of Philip II's Spain, financed by the silver of South America and fortified by the faith of the Counter-Reformation.

Palace of Charles V, Granada

The Emperor Charles V is one of the most underrated figures in European history, in spite of his obvious eminence as ruler of the greatest empire since the Romans. His talents were not showy; his brain, though sound, did not work fast, and in some fundamental respects he was old-fashioned – a chivalrous Burgundian knight in a world of ambitious, Machiavellian princes. Of all his dominions, he came to prefer Spain and that preference, arguably, had profound effects for the future of Europe.

As a newcomer to Spain he was deeply impressed by the magnificent Muslim palace of the Alhambra, in Granada, and when he came to build his own Spanish palace, he chose the same site. The two buildings now stand, virtually adjoining, on the same hill above the city.

Charles was not such a builder as his Valois rival in France, François I, and in fact his Granada palace was never completed. It is, nevertheless, one of the most impressive buildings of its date (1526). The architect was a Spaniard, Pedro Machuca, who had studied under Michelangelo and had acquired a sound comprehension of the Classical principles of the Italian Renaissance.

The palace is square in plan, about 60 metres (200 feet) along each side, and it stands around a splendid court, about 30 metres (100 feet) in diameter, which in its own way is as impressive as the courts of the Alhambra. Classical columns support colonnade and gallery, and the same two tiers of columns reappear on the outer façade. The building is two storeys high, with circular windows above the main windows, a device which not only looks effective from outside but also eases the always awkward problem of making floor levels match windows.

Royal Palace, Madrid

Madrid is not a particularly impressive capital in the architectural sense, at least by comparison with other great European capitals. One reason is that it is a comparatively new capital. The Emperor Charles V, who found its altitude soothed his chronic gout, spent long periods in Madrid and his son, Philip II, made it the Spanish capital about 1560. But it has remained a *villa* (town) rather than a *ciudad* (city).

The most impressive secular building is the royal palace, which stands on the site of the old Moorish alcazar. The original building, much altered in the 16th century, was damaged beyond repair by a fire in Christmas week, 1734, and Philip V took the opportunity of building a new palace in closer accord with Bourbon tastes. The original scheme was drawn up by the great Filippo Juvarra, but it was so immense that it was never carried out. After Juvarra's death in 1736, the project was taken over by his pupil, Giovanni Battista (Juan Bautista in Spain) Sacchetti (1700–64), whose major work it is. An imposing, almost overwhelming edifice, its great height was partly dictated by the

sloping site. Conforming to conventional North Italian Baroque style, it owes something to the Louvre in Paris but very little to native Spanish traditions, and it is built in a whitish granite which has the appearance of marble. Immense statues of past Spanish monarchs were created to stand on the balustrade, but when the time came to put them in place someone's nerve failed and, rather sadly, they were positioned less hazardously at ground level, around the Plaza de Oriente.

Overleaf: The garden façade of the Royal Palace in Madrid.

Charles V's Palace at Granada is rather lacking in historical atmosphere but is of considerable architectural interest; the proportions of the curved double colonnade are particularly admirable.

A detail of the surprising, extravagant Rococo decoration in the Sala de Gasperini, perhaps the most memorable apartment of the Royal Palace in Madrid.

The state rooms on the first floor, reached by a splendid Baroque staircase, contain many treasures. There is a porcelain room, its walls covered by yellow and green plaques, inspired no doubt by the slightly earlier porcelain room at Aranjuez. Here the decoration is Neo-Classical, but *chinoiserie* makes its appearance in the Sala de Gasperini, with its remarkable stucco ceiling, and in some other rooms. There are fine tapestries, some dating from the 15th century, a magnificent library, scintillating glass chandeliers, and ceilings painted by many of the great Spanish masters. The paintings in general are of a high quality but appear less impressive if you have spent the previous day in the Prado. The Armoury, south of the main palace complex, contains one of Europe's greatest collections of armour, including the suit worn by Charles V in the famous equestrian portrait by Titian.

Portugal

Queluz

The royal palace of Queluz stands on the main road from Lisbon to Sintra. It is the last great Rococo palace in Europe. Begun in 1747, it was still under construction during the great earthquake (1755) but seems to have suffered little. It consists of an irregular assembly of two-storey pavilions, linked by low, narrow wings. The stucco of the walls is a deep pink, with white stonework and lime-green frames for doors and windows. The interior was badly damaged by fire in 1934 but has since been restored.

Originally built for a younger son of the royal family, Queluz is an enchanting building which makes no effort to be imposing in the grand Baroque manner. The two architects chiefly responsible were Vicente de Oliveira and a Frenchman, J-B. Robillon. Oliveira's masterpiece is the central block, of modest but perfect proportions, which overlooks the elaborate hanging gardens. These were designed by Robillon in the French manner with extensive topiary by a Dutchman, Gerald van den Kolk, lead statues (originally painted) by an Englishman, John Cheeve, and a charming Dutch canal lined with tiles depicting maritime scenes.

Robillon's most notable work at Queluz is the western pavilion, an extraordinary little building reached by the dramatic Lions Staircase. The façade commences with a sober Classical colonnade and rises to a perfect riot of Rococo statuary against the sky. The design of the eastern pavilion, by an unknown architect, is in its own way equally remarkable, with its daring scrolled pediment.

The main rooms are the Sala des Mangas, with *azulejos* (decorative tiles) in the 'Chinese' taste, predominantly blue and gold; the Hall of Mirrors, glittering with glass and gilt; the subtly shaped Music Room, and the oval Ball Room, with

Overleaf: Queluz, the main façade. This highly attractive Rococo residence, which owed its existence to the recent discovery of gold in Brazil, was described by a Portuguese historian as 'the finest expression of the aristocratic society of the second half of the 18th century'.

The Sala de Mangas, which leads to the main state apartments at Queluz, is decorated with tile panels (*azulejos*) displaying the wealth of Portugal's overseas possessions.

The Ball Room, an elliptical oval, at Queluz. The pairs of herms in the corners seem rather intrusive; it has been suggested that they derive from the style of imperial Vienna, where Pombal, the virtual ruler of Portugal in the mid-18th century, had served a long spell as ambassador.

vast glass chandeliers and lavish gilding.

Sintra

The royal palace of Sintra, less than 30 kilometres from Lisbon, was badly damaged by the famous earthquake of 1755, but promptly restored to its original state. It contains a number of relics, including a marble seat from which Camoẽns recited the *Lusiads*, and a mosaic floor worn by the pacing of the deposed Alfonso VI.

From a great distance the palace might be mistaken for a Kentish oast house, as the two huge cone-shaped chimneys above the kitchens are the dominant feature. At close range, the effect of generations of additions justifies the verdict of the 18th-century English traveller, William Beckford: 'this confused pile'. Confused – and also confusing. Beckford, not to mention most modern guidebooks, supposed it was once a Moorish palace, but despite many Moorish aspects it is now thought to be later, and though founded on the site of a Moorish palace, contains nothing earlier than the reign of John I (1385–1433). It has many features exemplifying the distinctive Portuguese Late Gothic architectural style known as Manueline.

Perhaps the most attractive features of Sintra are the painted ceilings and the decorative tiles (*azulejos*). The Sala des Sereias, for example, has rare black tiles from the 15th century on the walls and on the ceiling a ship against a green sea filled with cavorting mermaids (maritime motifs were common at this period, the great age of Portuguese navigation). In the Sala dos Brasoẽs there are *azulejos* of pastoral scenes and a panelled ceiling of stags with the arms of 72 noble families. Another ceiling bears swans, in memory of the pets of the daughter of John I. The king's bedroom is tiled with raised green vine leaves which have reminded English visitors of Victorian Wedgwood.

The old palace of Sintra is not particularly elegant from the outside, and tends to be dominated by the enormous chimneys of the kitchen (just visible above the roof in this photograph).

Left: An example of the *azulejos* decoration, a favourite Portuguese device especially notable at Sintra.

Palaces of Denmark, Sweden and Holland

Denmark

Amalienborg

The area of Copenhagen traditionally known as Fredericksstaden is perhaps the most distinguished-looking quarter in the city. Its centre is the Amalienborg Plads, a broad space which must not be called a square as it is in fact octagonal, around which stand four separate palaces. They are more or less identical in outward appearance although the Brockdorff Palace, the present residence of the Danish monarch, can be distinguished from the others by its clock over the main entrance.

The present arrangement is the result of a remarkable piece of 18th-century town planning. In the 17th century a castle was built on the site for Sofie Amalie, queen of Frederik III, but it was burned down in 1689. In the 18th century, when many of the noble mansions in this part of Copenhagen were erected, the site was redeveloped in an original way, partly at least on the instigation of Frederik V. The plans of 1749 included the impressive Frederik-skirke (not completed until the late 19th century) whose lofty dome commands the area, and a central space, the Amalienborg Plads, with houses to be built by private interests under the control of the court architect, Nicolai Eigtved. Not surprisingly, this arrangement was found to be impracticable, and eventually Eigtved himself designed the buildings around the Plads.

The final result was the work of both Eigtved himself and of the German (but Italian-trained) architect, Marcus Tuscher, who was responsible for the traditional Baroque form of the palaces – a large main block flanked by pavilions. The palaces were then presented by the King to four of his most eminent subjects, on the condition that the façades should be built exactly according to plan (they were free to design the interiors as they wished).

The greatest of the four fortunate proprietors was undoubtedly Count von Moltke. It was his palace which Christian VII moved into in 1794, when the whole complex was taken over by the royal family after the palace of Charlottenborg had burned down, and it remains the grandest of the four today. The Riddersalen, or Barons' Hall, is one of the finest Rococo chambers outside France, with intricate gilded stucco, fine wood carvings, and paintings by that prince of the Rococo, François Boucher, who also designed the Beauvais tapestries in another part of the palace.

Christiansborg

Christiansborg, the royal *slot* (castle) in Copenhagen, is a striking example of permanence amid destruction. The present building is the sixth that has stood on this site, known as Slotsholm (castle island) across the canal near the Knippels bridge.

Here Axel Hvide, better known as Bishop Absalon, founder of the city, erected his *castrum de Hafn* in 1167. Commanding the harbour, it played

The Amalienborg, in Copenhagen, is the result of an enlightened piece of town planning in the 18th century.

an important part in the development of the little fishing and trading port during the Middle Ages. Its history was stormy. In the 13th century it was captured twice, destroyed and rebuilt. In the 14th century the Hanseatic League razed it to the ground, but it rose again and became a royal residence early in the 15th century. Under Christian III (reigned 1534–59) it was considerably enlarged and in the 17th century a tower was erected by Christian IV.

Frederick IV planned a thorough reconstruction in the 1720s, but it subsequently appeared that the old buildings were not worth preserving. Under Christian VI they were largely demolished and an entirely new structure, the first to be known as Christiansborg, was built between 1731 and 1745. This was the most splendid period in the history of the castle. The Rococo Christiansborg must have been a splendid place, judging by what remains – the

Christiansborg Castle has been rebuilt a remarkable number of times in the course of its stormy history, and much of it is less than a hundred years old. The unusual tower is a famous landmark in the Danish capital.

The stables of Christiansborg Castle house a famous riding school.

charming marble bridge with its two pavilions and some colonnades.

Unfortunately, most of it was destroyed by fire in 1794. It was rebuilt in Neo-Classical style by C. F. Hansen, but in 1884 this building suffered the same fate. The present palace, by Thorvald Jörgensen, founded as recently as 1907, contains the Danish parliament, supreme court and foreign ministry, as well as the monarch's official residence.

The building is of granite with a green copper roof and copper-sheathed tower of extravagant design, about 100 metres (330 feet) high. Most of the art treasures and furniture were rescued from the fire of 1884, including the bronze statues by H. V. Bissen which formerly crowned the portal. Some traces of the earlier buildings, including Bishop Absalon's castle, can still be seen.

Sweden

Drottningholm

Drottningholm, the summer residence of the Swedish monarchs on the island of Lovö, is a fine example of a Baroque palace inspired largely by French example, but much more modest than Versailles. It is especially attractive from the rear, where formal terraced gardens in the manner of André le Nôtre lead down to the open expanse of the lake.

A smaller building, about one hundred years old, already stood on the site when the decision was taken to build the present palace in the 1660s. The work was directed by members of three generations of the famous family of statesmen and architects, the Tessins, and the basic design is the work of Nicodemus Tessin the elder (father of the builder of the royal palace in Stockholm). Though the French influence is obvious in the arrangement of a central block with projecting wings,

Drottningholm is no slavish copy; Italian traditions also contributed and the ultimate effect is of an individual version of the Baroque.

The palace contains handsome rooms, with frescoes by the Swedish painter D. K. Ehrenstrahl, Gobelin tapestries and some remarkable furniture. In the grounds is a jolly little Rococo Chinese pavilion decorated by Jean Eric Rehn.

The most famous feature of Drottningholm is undoubtedly the theatre. The original theatre perished by fire in 1762, but its replacement is still one of the oldest theatres in Europe still used for plays and opera.

Drottningholm was at its most splendid during the eventful reign of that cultured monarch, Gustavus III (1771–92), and the disgruntled aristocrat who shot Gustavus also extinguished the brilliant court of Drottningholm. The palace fell into neglect – the theatre was used as a store-room – from which it was not rescued until the present century.

The garden façade, Drottningholm. This summer palace, a brilliant white in the sunshine, is a successful amalgam of Baroque styles, though the predominant influence is French.

Skokloster

In the 17th century Sweden achieved for the only time in its history the status of a great power. In particular, the military victories of Gustavus Adolphus in the Thirty Years' War astonished Europe. Among Sweden's other great commanders was Karl Gustav von Wrangel (1613–76). He was born on his father's estate near Uppsala, and in about 1750, as befitted such a great man, he built himself a palace close to the house in which he was born. It remains the finest private mansion in Sweden.

The architect was a Frenchman, Jean de la Vallée, and some of the decorative details were by German and Italian artists, but throughout the house the influence of the no-nonsense military proprietor can easily be sensed. Built as four sides of a square around a central courtyard, the house has four identical façades. Even the main entrance façade is only distinguished from the other three by a flight of steps and a pediment bearing the family coat of arms; the door itself is the same as the plain, arched windows, extended downwards to ground level. Each corner has a domed, octagonal tower.

Skokloster is now a museum, though the descendants of its original inhabitant lived there until very recently. It contains a famous collection of arms and armour, part of it amassed by Count Wrangel himself, a magnificent library, and flamboyant Baroque plasterwork, especially in the King's Room, originally the dining room, which derives its name from the portraits of Swedish kings hung around the walls.

Royal Palace, Stockholm

The royal palace, or *Slott*, of Stockholm has been called the finest monument to French art outside France. Though large, it is not as large as Versailles (the great exemplar in royal palaces) and certainly much less grand. However, the ascendancy of Sweden in the 17th century called for something more splendid than the ramshackle old castle which then occupied the site. The original plan was to alter and extend the castle, and much of this work had been started when the castle was destroyed by fire in 1697. The body of Charles XI, recently deceased, was barely rescued from the flames.

The new king, Charles XII, far more famous in European history but

Top: The ceremonial staircase at Drottningholm. The paintings are by a famous Swedish artist of the 17th century, D. K. Ehrenstrahl, for whom one of the rooms is named.

Above: The state bedchamber at Drottningholm, with the bed set in an alcove, was originally decorated in blue and gold for King Gustavus III.

far less desirable as a ruler, was hostile to all things French and needed all available cash for his sensational military campaigns. Early casualties were the statues which should have surmounted the pediment of the palace in the Versailles manner, leaving the outline rather stark. Construction of the palace itself was temporarily halted in 1710, Charles's wars having emptied the exchequer, but work resumed about 1728 and the building was completed by 1754, though altered since then.

In appearance, the Swedish royal palace, consisting of a large quadrangular block with extending wings on either side, is somewhat severe; it owes as much to the great *palazzi* of Renaissance Italy as to the French Baroque. The interior, however, is in the French style, mainly of the Louis XV period, and indeed was largely designed and executed by French craftsmen, some of whom would certainly be more famous if they had stayed in France instead of spending their working lives in Sweden. Many of the furnishings, including Savonnerie carpets and tapestries designed by François Boucher, were imported direct from Paris, while others are the work of Carl Hårleman and Jean Eric Rehn, both French-trained, who successively superintended the works in the 18th century.

Above: Skokloster Castle now belongs to the state and there is a 'vacation centre' in the grounds. This pleasingly symmetrical country palace was for most of its history in the possession of the Brahe family, relatives of Count Wrangel who died without direct heirs.

Left: In the 17th century Sweden was one of the greatest powers in Europe, and the grandeur of the Royal Palace in Stockholm reflects the stature of imperial Sweden.

Holland

Royal Palace, Amsterdam

The royal palace of Amsterdam stands on the west side of the Dam, the heart of the city from which major streets radiate. It is rectangular in plan, measuring about 93 × 75 metres (305 × 245 feet), and is an example of Dutch 17th-century civic architecture in the Classical or Palladian style. The façades are simple and uncluttered by ornament except for the sculpture in the pediment and on the capitals of the pilasters which march, in two tiers, across the building. Only the tall cupola above the pediment makes any suggestion of a departure from strict and sober Classicism.

The building dates from the close of the Thirty Years' War in 1648, the period when the Dutch, free from Spanish rule and not yet in conflict with England, reached the height of their commercial and maritime prosperity. Everything about the palace, from the weather vane in the form of a Dutch cog or merchant ship (the badge of the city) to the hand-

A striking pair of bronze gates in the Royal Palace of Amsterdam. (Photo: Bart Hofmeester.)

The elegant, vaulted Hall of Moses, who can be seen admonishing the Israelites in the painting at the left, in the Royal Palace, Amsterdam. The Dutch tended to identify the Israelites' escape from Egypt with their own escape from Spanish rule. (Photo: Bart Hofmeester.)

some chimneypieces within, suggests a wealthy community of burghers, confident, satisfied, and wealthy. So it should, for the palace was originally built as the city hall (an earlier one having burned down). It retained that function until 1808, when Louis Bonaparte, brother of Napoleon and King of Holland from 1806 to 1810, ordered its conversion.

The architect was Jacob van Campen, the foremost Dutch architect of the day, with some contributions by Daniel Stalpaert. The sculpture of the pediment, representing the Merchant City surrounded by Neptune, tritons and sea nymphs, is by Artus Quellin the elder, member of a notable family of sculptors.

The most remarkable room is the spacious great hall, which stands without the aid of supplementary supports. The walls, like those of many other rooms, are faced with white marble and the floor is inlaid with a representation of the heavens in copper. Amsterdam herself again appears in allegorical guise, accompanied by figures of Strength, Plenty and Wisdom.

The Royal Palace in the centre of Amsterdam, though handsome enough, suggests its origins as a civic building rather than a royal residence.

Huis ten Bosch

Huis ten Bosch, 'House of the Woods', is the old country house of the princes of Orange, near the Hague. It is essentially a pleasantly unpretentious villa, one of the few royal residences one would actually like to live in. The original palace was built about 1645 for the Stadtholder, Frederick Henry, possibly the most accomplished of the princes of Orange, and his wife, Princess Amalia. When Frederick Henry died in 1647, she turned it into a memorial, and it was known as the Oranjesael. It was a single block with, on the main façade, a Classical portico flanked by projecting wings. On the shorter sides the triple motif was repeated but with the central portion

Above right: Without its dome, Huis ten Bosch would look like little more than a pleasant mansion inhabited, possibly, by a wealthy stockbroker or an old people's home. Its history and interior decoration qualify it as a 'palace'. (Photo: Bart Hofmeester.)

Right: An elegantly furnished room in Huis ten Bosch in which Neo-Classical design is lightened by some Rococo touches. (Photo: Bart Hofmeester.)

projecting over a colonnade. The main feature, apart from the entrance, was a domed octagon. Inside, a large central hall rose nearly the whole height of the building.

The palace was enlarged for Prince William IV in the 18th century by Daniel Marot, who added sympathetic flanking wings and altered the octagon and lantern, as well as redesigning the interior.

Besides massive symbolic paintings celebrating the House of Orange by 17th-century Dutch artists such as Gerard van Honthorst, the palace contains several very charming rooms, including a Chinese Room and a Japanese Room, added in the 19th century. The White Dining Room, one of the few survivals of Marot's interior scheme, is perhaps the most attractive, with an accomplished vaulted stucco ceiling in the Rococo style (the single most famous feature of the palace), augmented by a chandelier of Waterford glass and contemporary grisailles by Jacob de Witt.

The Napoleonic period was one of decline for the palace; subsequently it regained its proper role as a country residence for the Dutch royal family. The attractive gardens mostly date from the 19th century.

Marot's stucco vaulted ceiling is the best-known feature of the decoration at Huis ten Bosch. (Photo: Bart Hofmeester.)

Palaces of the U.S.S.R. and Central Europe

U.S.S.R.

Grand Kremlin Palace, Moscow

The Kremlin, or citadel, in Moscow occupied a site of some nine acres and includes a large number of churches, palaces and towers. The Kremlin is still (as everyone knows) the political and administrative centre of the Soviet Union, though most of its historic buildings have been converted into museums. During the 1830s Tsar Nicolas I commissioned a large new palace to replace the somewhat cluttered earlier buildings and provide suitable quarters for himself and his court during visits to Moscow. The old palace complexes were demolished (except for the 17th-century Terem and two other buildings) to make way for the Grand Kremlin Palace, which was completed in 1849.

At this period there was a conscious revival of a 'national' style, expressing a desire to return to Russia's glorious traditions in the wake of the Napoleonic invasion (in which much of Moscow was destroyed). The architect of the enormous new palace was Konstantin Thon, and his attempt to revitalize traditional Russian style is most obvious in the design of the windows and the ogee curves in which the pilasters terminate on the façade which looks out over the Moscow River.

The three-storeyed building, in yellow and white, is covered by an iron roof, and the main façade centres on a curious, tent-like, pedimental construction. The iron stanchions were designed by a professor at Moscow University. The building is said to be able to accommodate 20,000 people, large enough, surely, even for the Romanov court, and there are about 700 separate apartments, all of them furnished in a luxurious manner. In the elaborate Hall of St George, marble plaques commemorate Russian military heroes, and the Hall of St Vladimir gives access to the old Terem palace, a building which recalls the traditional wooden architecture of Russia.

Thon also built the Church of the Redeemer in the Kremlin and the Armoury Palace (1849–51), a picturesque 19th-century version of the Renaissance style, which to most people is a more successful building than the barbaric bulk of the Grand Kremlin Palace. Today it contains

Overleaf: A view of the Kremlin from across the river in Moscow. The vast bulk of the Grand Kremlin Palace fronts the river. To the right arise the gilded cupolas of the Kremlin cathedrals.

The intricate design of balustrade and capitals relieves the general severity of a hall of the Grand Kremlin Palace.

the finest collection of Russian treasures in Moscow, consisting of armour, gold and silver, jewellery, costume, etc. There you can see the helmet worn by the father of Alexander Nevsky, the gold throne of Boris Godunov, a carriage presented by Elizabeth I of England, and the tsars' equestrian trappings, worn by an alarmingly realistic horse.

Tsarskoe Selo

The Great Palace of Catherine the Great at Tsarskoe Selo near Leningrad (originally St Petersburg), began life as a country estate which Peter the Great gave to his wife. The original house was reconstructed for the Empress Elizabeth by the Italian architect, Bartolommeo Rastrelli, with the help of craftsmen from all over Russia and labourers recruited from the army. Rastrelli's style was,

despite both his origin and place of work, predominantly French in character, and his two Franco-Russian masterpieces are the Winter Palace and this building.

Tsarksoe Selo (village of the tsars) is built around a colossal quadrangle, and is almost as large as the Winter Palace and, on the whole, even more decorative. The main façade, approximately 100 metres (330 feet) long, in blue, white and gold, is adorned with columns, pilasters, balustrades, Atlantes and broken pediments which, as in the Winter Palace, interrupt the immense vista with light and shade, and give a sense of powerful rhythm.

Of Rastrelli's interiors, few survive today. Under Catherine the Great, considerable alterations were effected by the Scottish architect, Charles Cameron, who subdued some of the

Catherine the Great's Palace at Tsarskoe Selo (Pushkin) near Leningrad bears a marked resemblance to the Winter Palace, with its heavily articulated façade. The drainpipes in this photograph tend to invite ironic comment on Soviet practicality.

Overleaf: Rastrelli's façade for the Winter Palace on the Neva at Leningrad seems to march along for ever. In order to make the building blend in with the rest of the city, Rastrelli was limited to a height of only 20 metres (65 feet), though the length is nearly 150 metres (495 feet). The result is a considerable success; there is no suggestion of dwarfishness.

Left: A detail of the Empress's bedroom at Tsarskoe Selo, with decoration by Charles Cameron which includes inlaid Wedgwood plaques, specially manufactured.

Below: Cameron's elegant Green Dining Room at Tsarskoe Selo.

Rococo exuberance with his own elegant brand of Neo-Classicism. He was, of course, a countryman and contemporary of Robert Adam, the prince of Neo-Classicism in England, but Cameron's plasterwork, as seen in the Green Dining Room for instance, is much more elaborate. His interiors at Tsarskoe Selo are among his finest work: he employed rich but delicate materials, with frequent use of glass, and his colours are predominantly pale, milky shades.

Some further alterations to the palace were made later, but they were insignificant compared with the disasters – looting and burning – of World War II. Since then the palace has been magnificently restored.

The Winter Palace, Leningrad
The Winter Palace in Leningrad is now incorporated in the great Hermitage Museum. Perhaps the

most memorable incident affecting this former palace of the tsars was its storming during the Russian Revolution, an event comparable in its symbolic significance with the storming of the Bastille.

The Winter Palace is a very large building, nearly 150 metres (495 feet) on its longer sides, and to some people it suggests the excesses of grand opera. However, the highly ornamental exterior and the way in which the extreme length of the two main façades is broken up by a double tier of columns are on the whole effective in counteracting the dangers of monotony. The original building was insignificant by comparison, but although that first Winter Palace was built in 1711, the present one is very largely a 19th-century structure.

As part of his policy of modernizing Russia, Peter the Great founded a new capital, St Petersburg, to give Russia a 'window on Europe', with a royal palace on the banks of the

mighty Neva. Nothing remains of this building, for it was replaced about ten years later, and the Winter Palace has since been completely rebuilt on three occasions, growing larger each time. Its greatness dates from the reign of the Empress Elizabeth (1741–62), when the architect in charge was an Italian, Bartolommeo Rastrelli, but work continued in the reign of Catherine the Great and throughout the 19th century, so that comparatively little is left of Rastrelli's admirable Rococo interiors.

A fire in the 1830s made much rebuilding necessary; the state rooms have been restored to their original condition (or, at any rate, something very like it) with gorgeous velvets and marbles, while the exterior is relatively unchanged except for its colour. The present pale green and white seems a preferable scheme to the dark reddish shade of the 19th century or even, perhaps, the orange and white specified by Rastrelli.

A ceremonial staircase in the Winter Palace (well travelled by Soviet citizens), which displays to the full the splendid theatricality of Rastrelli's Baroque style.

An airy, almost tent-like effect is achieved in the 'pavilion' room of the Winter Palace, and the Baroque of the original designer can be seen to be giving way to a more sober Neo-Classicism.

Czechoslovakia

Hradčany Castle

The great complex of buildings on the Hradčany hill in Prague, dominated by the splendid Gothic cathedral of St Vitus, has been the centre of Czech history for a thousand years. There was a wooden fortress on the site early in the 9th century, and the original Romanesque cathedral was begun by the monarch known as Good King Wenceslaus in the 10th century. In the 11th century the first stone castle was built. It was enlarged and reconstructed in succeeding centuries, but the greatest age of rebuilding was the reign of the Emperor Charles IV (Charles I of Bohemia), whose name is commemorated in the university and the famous bridge of Prague.

Under the direction of Matthew of Arras and Peter Parler (the most famous member of a great family of German masons in the 14th century), Hradčany Castle was almost completely rebuilt, along with St Vitus's Cathedral. Subsequently, the main periods of rebuilding were the early 16th century and the 18th century, when during the reign of Maria Theresa the present façade of the

Overleaf: The Mathias Gates of Hradčany Castle, with vigorous bronze statues of giants by I. F. Platzer commanding the courtyard.

palace was built by Nicolo Pacassi, conferring a certain uniformity on the picturesque assembly of buildings though in itself merely a rather conventional Baroque design, which is dull by comparison with other Baroque buildings in Prague.

Perhaps the most famous room in the castle is the Vladislav Hall, a magnificent late Gothic chamber on the second storey, used since its construction in 1486–1502 for various state ceremonies. It is an outstanding example of the work of a genius of the Late Gothic style, Benedikt Rejt, the curving ribs of the vault forming a sophisticated, almost plant-like pattern. There are other examples of richly decorative vaulting, for instance in the bedchamber of Vladislav Jagellon, also probably designed by Rejt but more conventional in form, and in the old Diet Hall.

Among early medieval remnants are the Romanesque basilica of St George, with its twin towers, and the great square mass of the Black Tower, lower down the hill. At a greater distance, you can see the curved green roof of the handsome summer palace, an attractive late-Renaissance building in the Italian style, designed by Paolo della Stella.

Vladislav Hall, the best-known work of Benedikt Rejt (or Rieth), in which Gothic and Renaissance forms mingle and a touch of innovative genius helps create a unique chamber.

Poland

Wawel Castle

The Wawel Castle, sited on a hill dominating the city of Cracow, is in essence a Polish medieval castle turned into an Italian Renaissance palace. The total effect is surprisingly harmonious despite some odd components, such as the little tent-like pavilion that rests on a convenient Gothic battlement, and the quaint Gothic pavilion known as the Hen's Foot.

In the 16th century Cracow was the capital of Poland, and the royal palace was largely built by Italians between 1507 and 1536. A central courtyard is surrounded by three-storey blocks with steepish roofs and distinctive, double-stage arcades surmounted by a colonnade, the height of which is equal to the two arcades below. Strangely, one of the four blocks surrounding the court-yard is, in effect, a dummy; containing no habitable rooms, it was erected for the sake of symmetry.

Some of the state rooms were decorated with considerable splendour. The Senate Chamber has magnificent Flemish tapestries illustrating the story of Noah, while the ceiling of the Chamber of Deputies is famous for its panels inset with realistically carved and painted heads. Throughout the palace, which is now a museum with an especially notable collection of armour, there are fine wooden doorways carved in the Late Gothic style, some interesting paintings and furniture, and attractive tiled stoves which still heat some of the rooms. The cathedral, in which Polish kings were crowned, adjoins the palace. It contains many royal tombs, including a fine effigy of Casimir the Great (1333–70), in pink marble, and a large Baroque mausoleum of St Stanislaus, patron saint of Poland.

The Wawel's most splendid period as the heart of the Polish nation was brief. In 1596 the capital was transferred to Warsaw, and the Wawel entered upon less fortunate times.

A distant view of Wawel Castle and the cathedral from the bridge over the Vistula.

Glossary

Atlantes The male form of **caryatids.**

Azulejos (Portuguese) Decorative ceramic tiles.

Baroque The style in art and architecture from the end of the 16th to the early 18th century (depending on country or region), employing basically Classical forms, treated in a freer, more expansive way; characterized by elaborate decoration, a sense of sweeping scale and movement and complex architectural schemes.

Caryatids Columns in the form of carved female figures, often used of a half-figure or **herm.**

Chinoiserie Decoration in the Chinese style, especially popular in the 18th century.

Classical Following the principles of ancient Greek or Roman architecture; Classical revivals, ie efforts to return to the basic rules and orders of antiquity, occurred periodically, notably during the Renaissance and in the late 18th century, when the movement was known as Neo-Classical.

Corbels Projecting stone blocks, often decoratively carved, which support a beam, vault, floor, etc.

Cornice A projecting ornamental moulding on the top of a wall, arch, etc; in **Classical** architecture, the topmost element of the **entablature.**

Corps de logis (French) The main buildings or central block.

Cortile (Italian) An interior courtyard, normally surrounded by an arcade.

Donjon (French) Equivalent to the English keep (of a castle).

Enfilade (French) The custom of arranging internal doors to give a view through several rooms.

Entablature In Classical architecture, the horizontal element above the columns, consisting of architrave, frieze and **cornice.**

Flamboyant The Late Gothic style in France, with ribs and tracery in wavy lines, like a flame (*flambeau*).

Grisaille Painting in tones of grey, popular on 18th-century murals and porcelain.

Hammerbeam A projecting beam at the top of a wall which supports the roof or vault and creates a narrower span.

Herm Strictly, a bust on a pedestal; sometimes incorporated in late Renaissance and Baroque buildings.

Lantern The decorative vertical structure on top of a dome or cupola.

Loggia (Italian) An arcaded gallery.

Mannerist The style bridging the Renaissance and the Baroque, in Italy especially, often comprising deliberate exaggeration of forms.

Mansard roof The lower part of the roof sloping more steeply than the upper part.

Manueline The distinctive Late Gothic style of Portugal, named after King Manuel (1495–1521), highly elaborate, characterized by twisted columns and luxuriant surface decoration.

Mukkarnas In Islamic architecture, pendant elements like stalactites in a vault.

Mullions Vertical elements that divide a window into two or more 'lights'.

Ogee An inward-outward curve, like a slender S.

Parterre (French) A formal arrangement of flower beds and paths.

Piano nobile (Italian) The principal floor, on the second storey, containing the chief apartments.

Pier A solid mass of stone functioning like a column, often applied to any supporting pillar which is not round in section.

Pilaster A pier-like form attached to a wall and projecting a comparatively short distance from it.

Putti (Italian) Chubby nude boys or cherubs, popular in Baroque decor.

Quoins Cornerstones at the angle formed by two walls, often staggered (one long, one short, etc), sometimes applied to similar treatment of windows and doors.

Rococo The culminating phase of Baroque, lighter, more curvy and colourful, often asymmetrical, with motifs based on seashells, etc, originating in France; more significant in decoration than architecture.

Roundel A circular plaque, often with a human head, badge, or other motif in relief.

Rusticated In walls, large stone blocks whose borders are emphasized by cutting away the edges; usually adopted for the wall of the lower storeys.